UKULELE TAB

15 GREAT PERFORMANCES TRANSCRIBED NOTE FOR NOTE

Music transcriptions by Pete Billmann

ISBN 978-1-4768-2253-2

7777 W. Bluemound Rd. P.O. Box 13819 Milwaukee, WI 53213

Visit Hal Leonard Online at
www.halleonard.com

from Troy Fernandez - *Hawaiian Style Ukulele*

Blue Hawaii

from the Paramount Picture WAIKIKI WEDDING
Theme from the Paramount Picture BLUE HAWAII

Words and Music by Leo Robin and Ralph Rainger

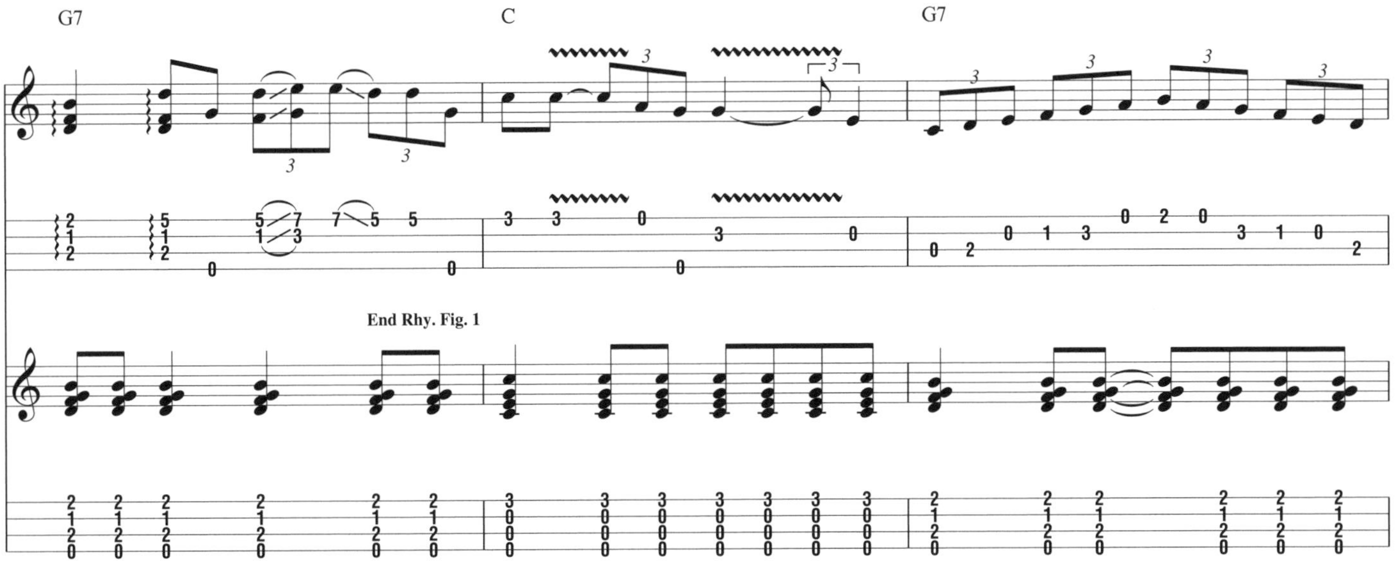
G7
C
G7
End Rhy. Fig. 1

Uke 2: w/ Rhy. Fig. 1
Uke 1
C
F
C

Dm
G7

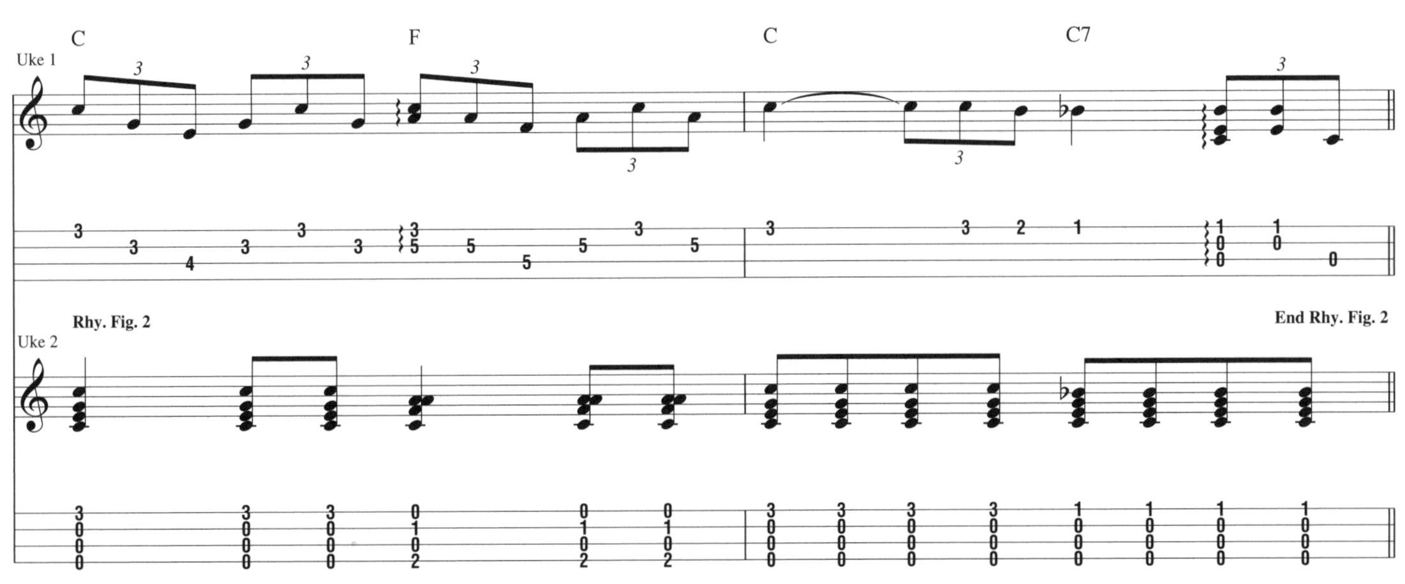
Uke 1
C
F
C
C7
Rhy. Fig. 2
Uke 2
End Rhy. Fig. 2

C
F
C
Rhy. Fig. 3
A7
D7
Dm
A♭7
G7
End Rhy. Fig. 3

D
Uke 2: w/ Rhy. Fig. 1
Uke 1
C
F
C
Dm
G7
Uke 2: w/ Rhy. Fig. 2
C
F
C
C7
E
Uke 2: w/ Rhy. Fig. 3
F
C
A7
D7
Dm
A♭7
G7

F

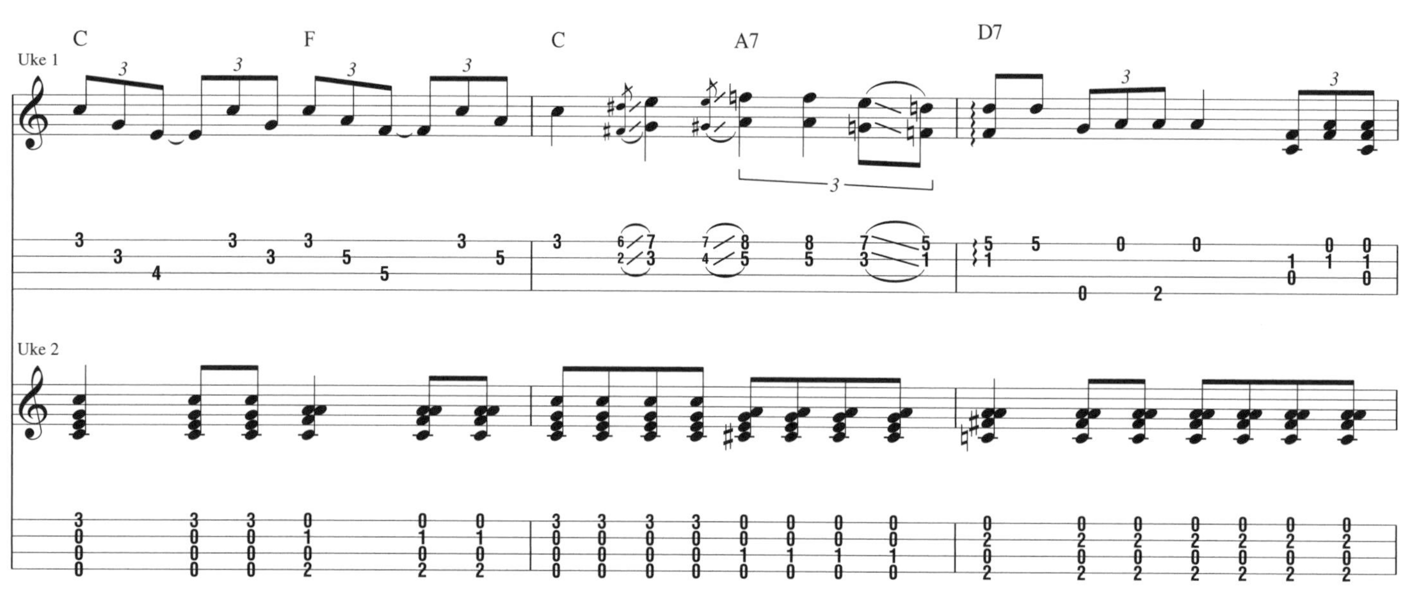

from Herb Ohta, Jr. - *Ukulele Breeze*

Europa (Earth's Cry Heaven's Smile)

Words and Music by Carlos Santana and Tom Coster

A tempo
Am
rit.
A tempo
E7
rit.
rit.
A tempo
Am
rit.
B
Slowly ♩ = 74
N.C.
Dm7
G7
Cmaj7
Fmaj7
Bm7♭5
E7
Am
Amaj7
Am
Dm9

G7
Cmaj7
Fmaj7

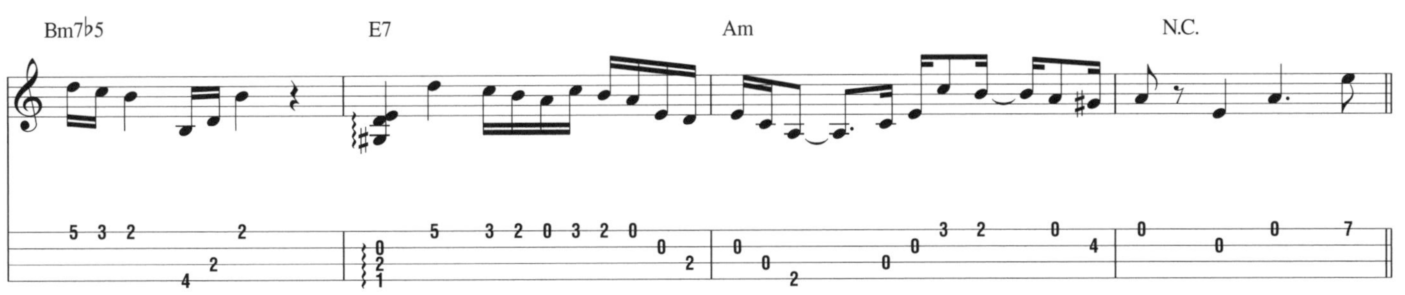
Bm7♭5
E7
Am
N.C.

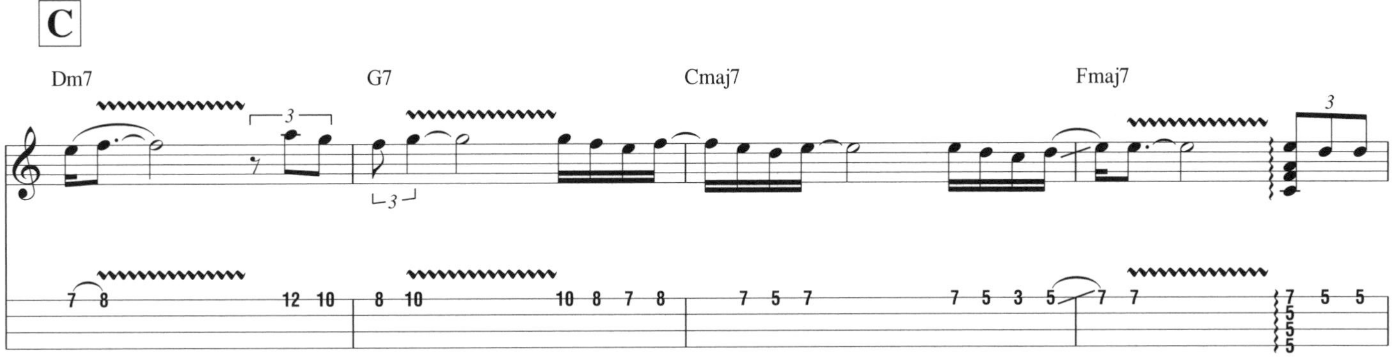
C
Dm7
G7
Cmaj7
Fmaj7

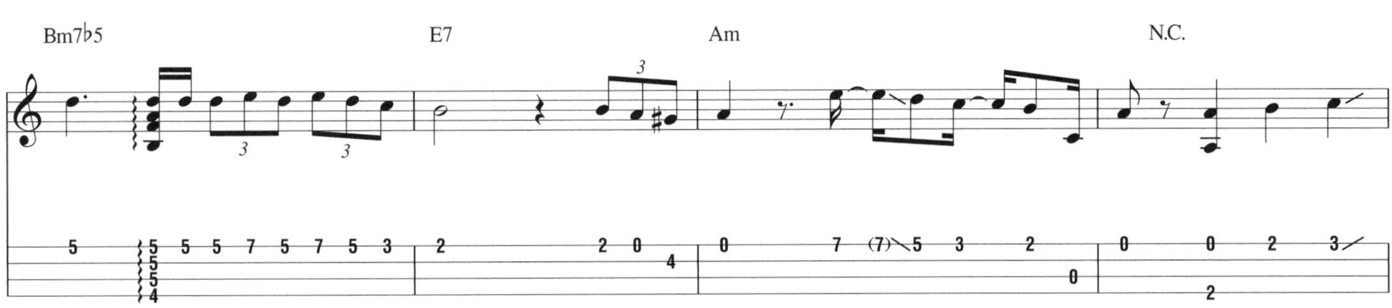
Bm7♭5
E7
Am
N.C.

Dm7/G
G7
Cmaj7
Fmaj7

To Coda

Bm7♭5
E7
Am

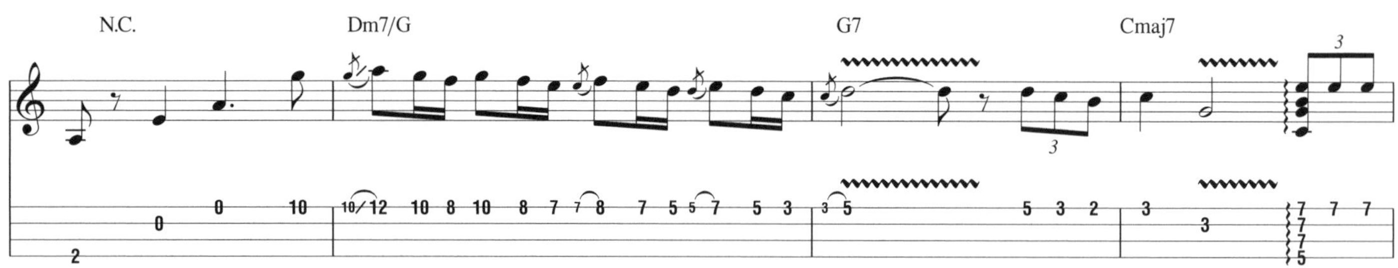
N.C.
Dm7/G
G7
Cmaj7

Fmaj7
Bm7♭5
E7
Am

N.C.
Dm7
G7

Cmaj7
Fmaj7
Bm7♭5

D.S. al Coda
E7
Am
N.C.

Coda

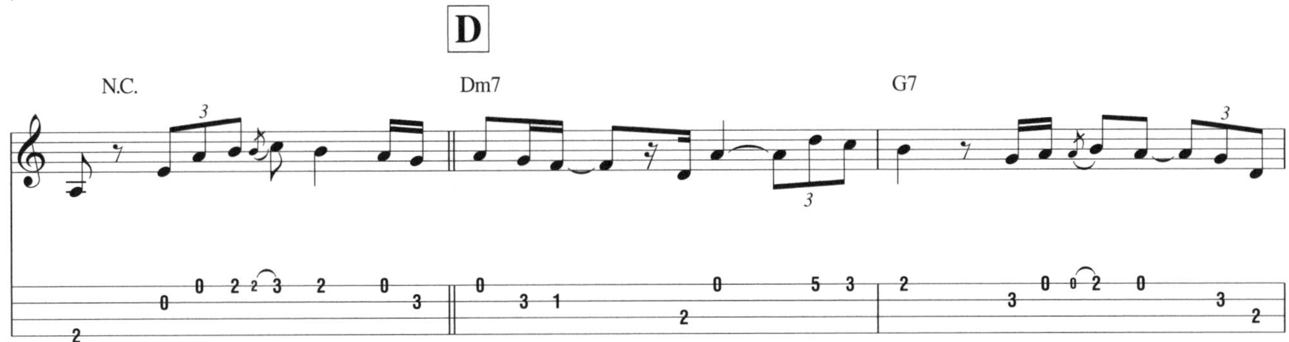
D
N.C.
Dm7
G7

Cmaj7
Fmaj7

Free time
E7
rit.
p

N.C.
Tempo 1
Am
mf

Am6
mp
mf

from Noah & The Whale - *Peaceful, The World Lays Me Down*

5 Years Time

By Charlie Fink

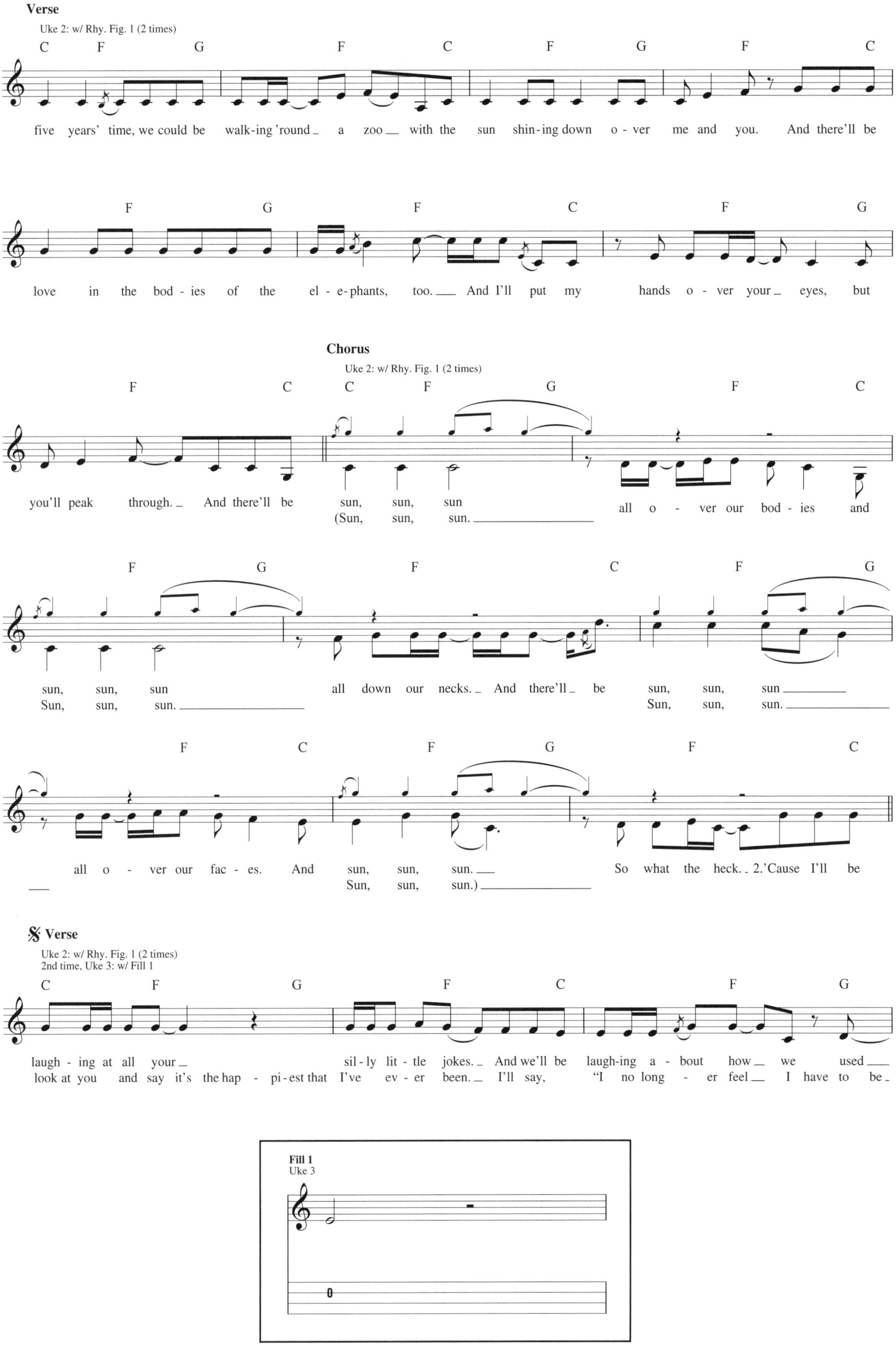

Verse

Uke 2: w/ Rhy. Fig. 1 (2 times)

C F G F C F G F C

five years' time, we could be walk-ing 'round _ a zoo _ with the sun shin-ing down o - ver me and you. And there'll be

F G F C F G

love in the bod - ies of the el - e-phants, too. _ And I'll put my hands o - ver your _ eyes, but

Chorus

Uke 2: w/ Rhy. Fig. 1 (2 times)

F C C F G F C

you'll peak through. _ And there'll be sun, sun, sun all o - ver our bod - ies and
(Sun, sun, sun. _

F G F C F G

sun, sun, sun all down our necks. _ And there'll _ be sun, sun, sun _
Sun, sun, sun. _ Sun, sun, sun. _

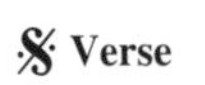
Verse

Uke 2: w/ Rhy. Fig. 1 (2 times)
2nd time, Uke 3: w/ Fill 1

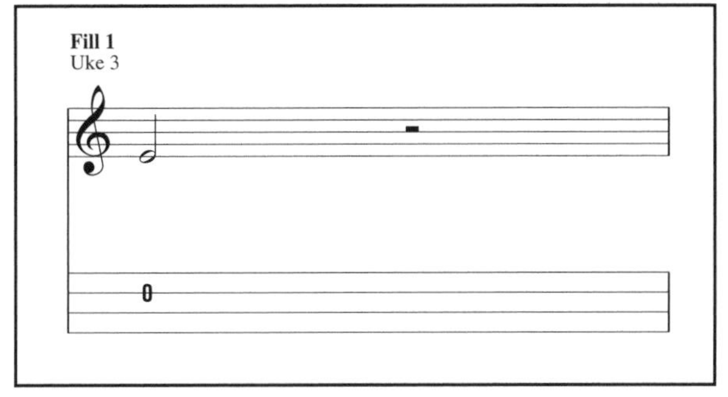

*Flute arr. for uke.

Coda
Verse
Uke 2 tacet
C F G F
me - di - ate - ly all these mo - ments are just in my head, I'll be
Uke 3
Rhy. Fig. 2
Uke 1
Uke 2
C F G F
think - ing 'bout them as I'm ly - ing in bed. And I know
Uke 3
Uke 1
End Rhy. Fig. 2
Uke 1: w/ Rhy. Fig. 2
C F G F C F
that im - me-di-ate-ly they might not e - ven come true, but in my mind I'm hav - in' a pret-ty good
Uke 3

Chorus

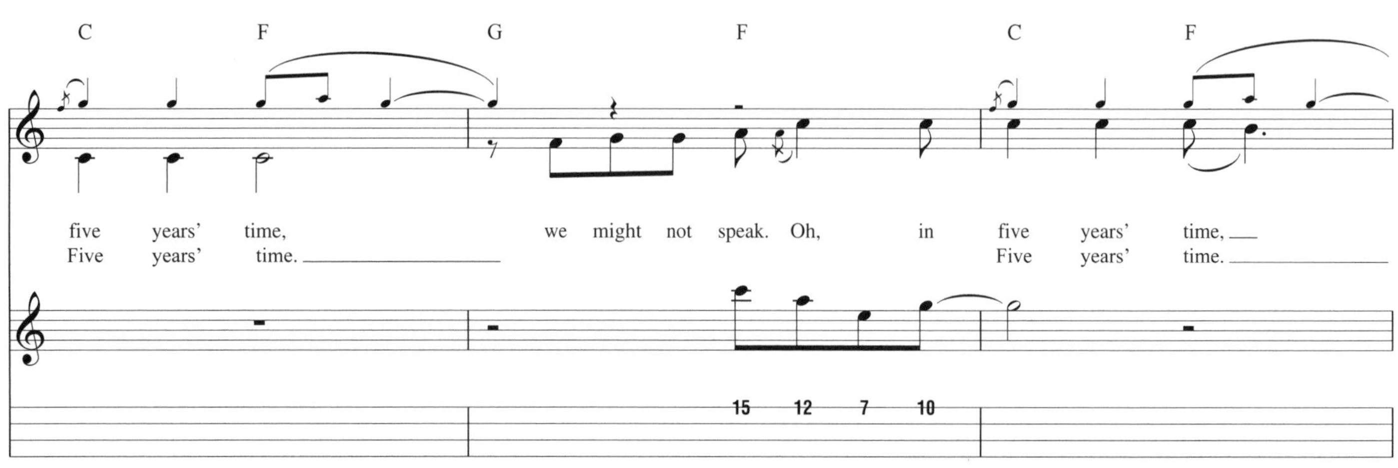

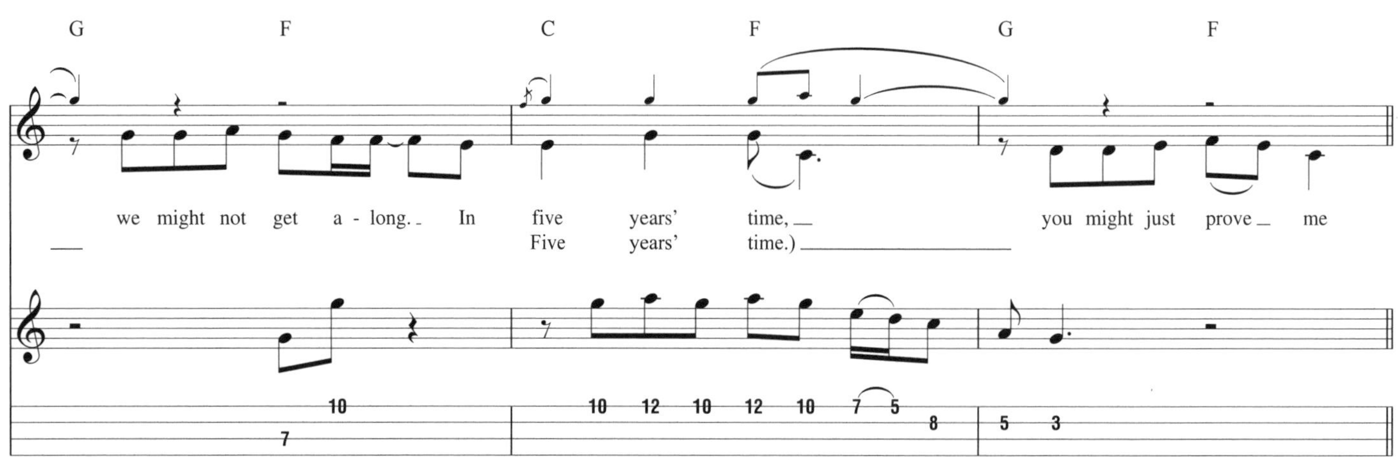

Interlude

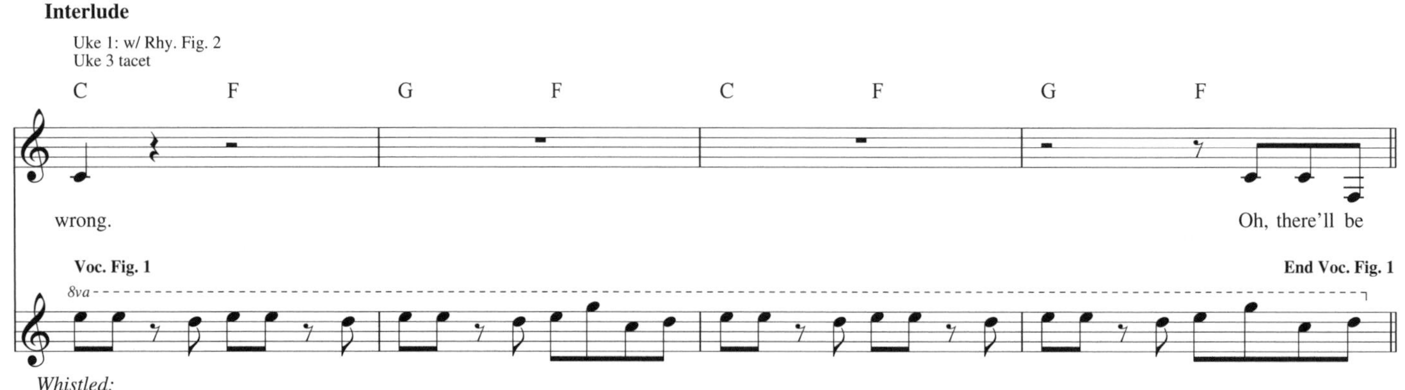

Bridge
Bkgd. Voc.: w/ Voc. Fig. 1 (1 3/4 times)
Uke 1 tacet
C
N.C.
love, love, love where-ev - er you go. There'll be love, love, love wher - ev - er you go. There'll be
Uke 1
love, love, love wher - ev - er you go. There'll be love, love, love wher - ev - er you go. There'll be
Outro-Chorus
Uke 2: w/ Rhy. Fig. 1 (1 1/2 times)
C F G F C F G
love, love, love wher - ev - er you go. There'll be love, love, love
(Love, love, love. Love, love, love.
F C F G F C
wher - ev - er you go. There'll be love, love love wher - ev - er you go. There'll be
Love, love, love.
F G F C
love, love, love wher - ev - er you go. There'll be love.
Love, love, love.)
Uke 2

from Troy Fernandez - *Hawaiian Style Ukulele, Vol. 2*

Hotel California

Words and Music by Don Henley, Glenn Frey and Don Felder

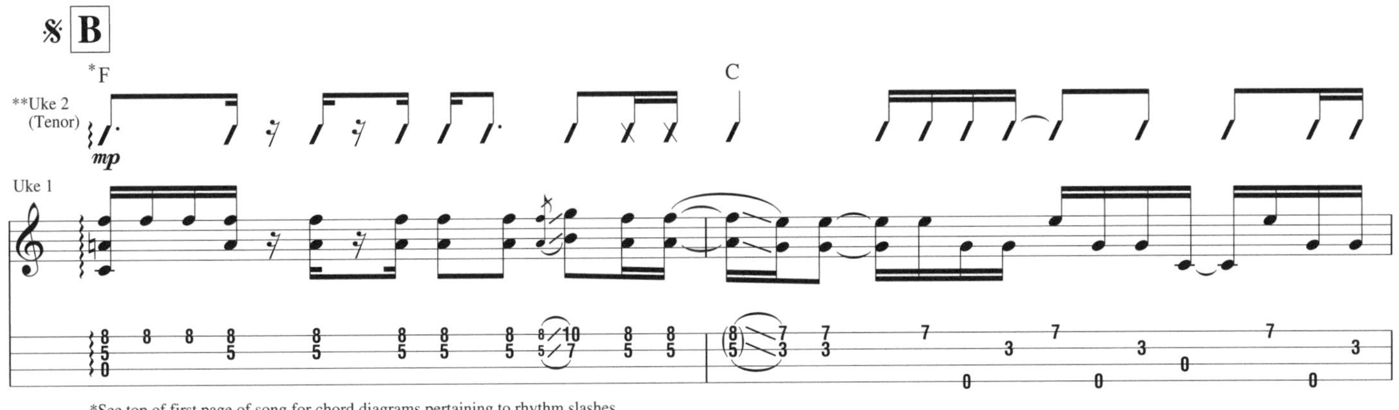

*See top of first page of song for chord diagrams pertaining to rhythm slashes.

**w/ low G 4th string.

Dm Am

F C

To Coda Dm E7

C

Am E7 G

Rhy. Fig. 1

D7
F
C
Dm
E7
End Rhy. Fig. 1
D
Uke 2: w/ Rhy. Fig. 1
Uke 1
Am
E7
G
D7
F
C
D.S. al Coda
Dm
E7

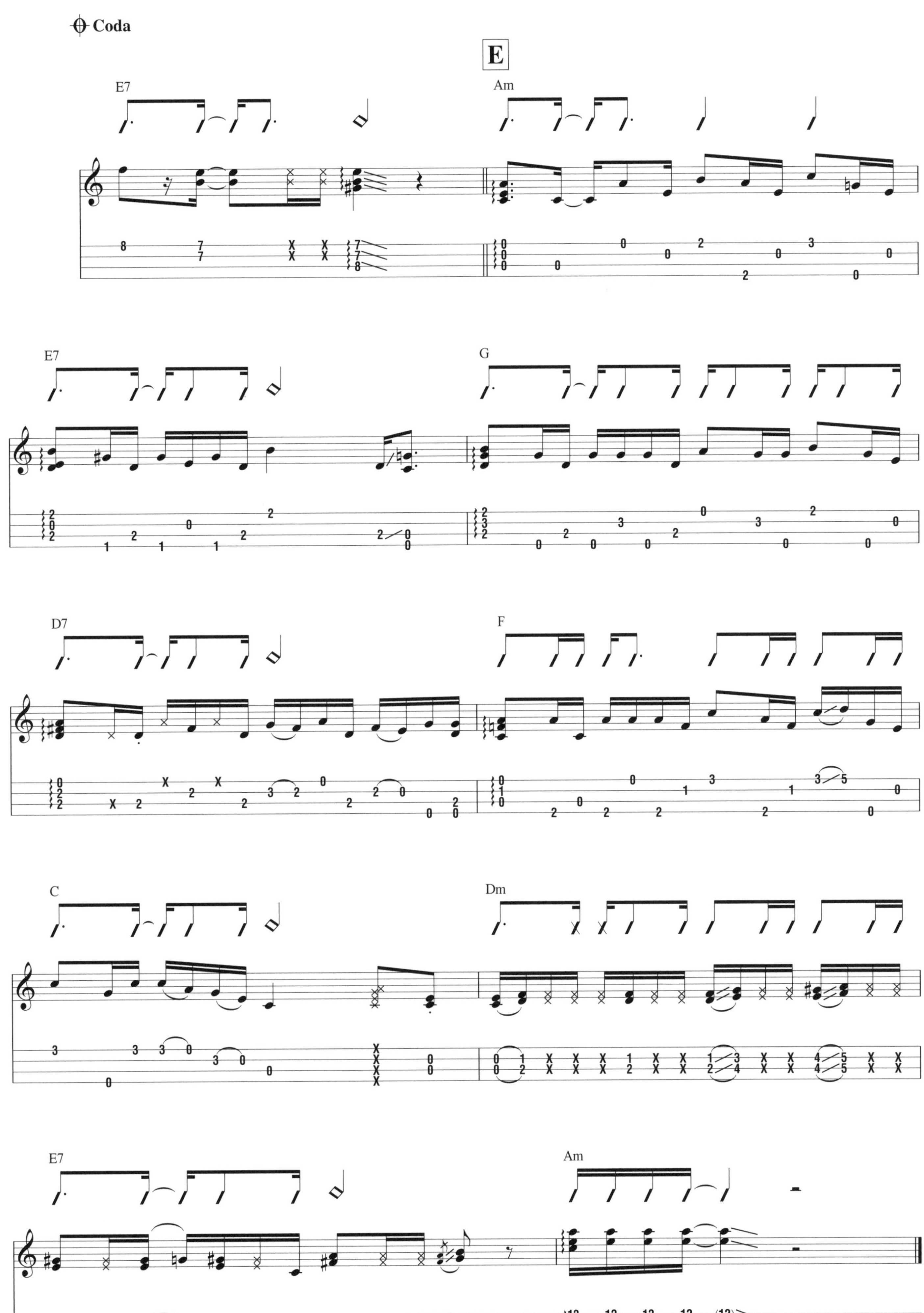
Coda
E
E7
Am
E7
G
D7
F
C
Dm
E7
Am

from Joe Brown - *The Ukulele Album*

I'll See You in My Dreams

Words by Gus Kahn
Music by Isham Jones

Am
E7
Am
Soon my eyes will close;
soon I'll find re - pose.
C
C♯°7
Dm
G7
C
Cmaj7
C7
And in dreams, you're al-ways near to me.
I'll
Chorus
B♭
B♭m6
see you in my dreams,
Rhy. Fig. 2
F
F6
C+
F6
hold you in my dreams.
End Rhy. Fig. 2

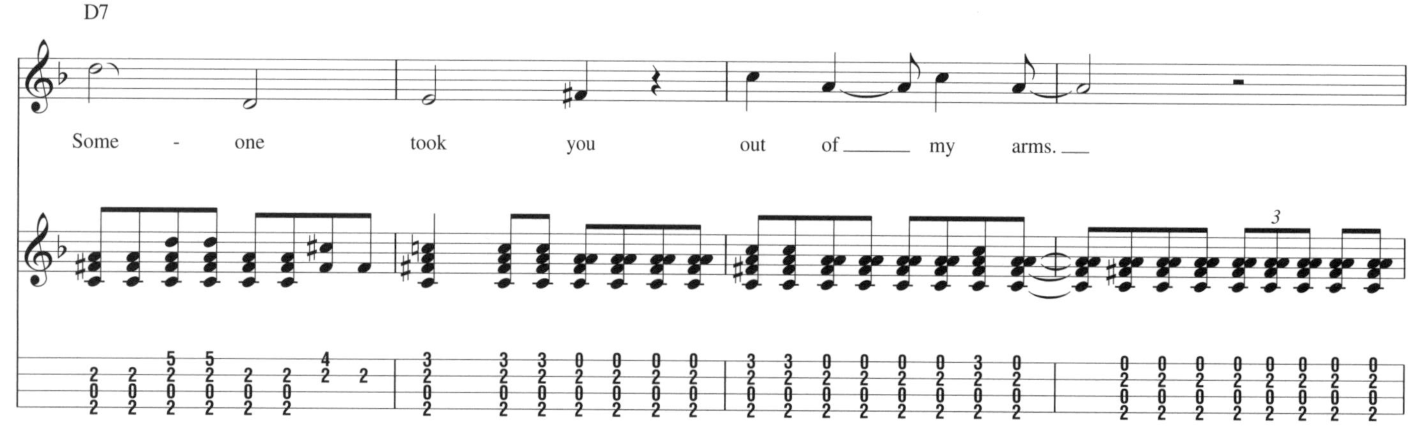
D7
Some - one took you out of my arms.

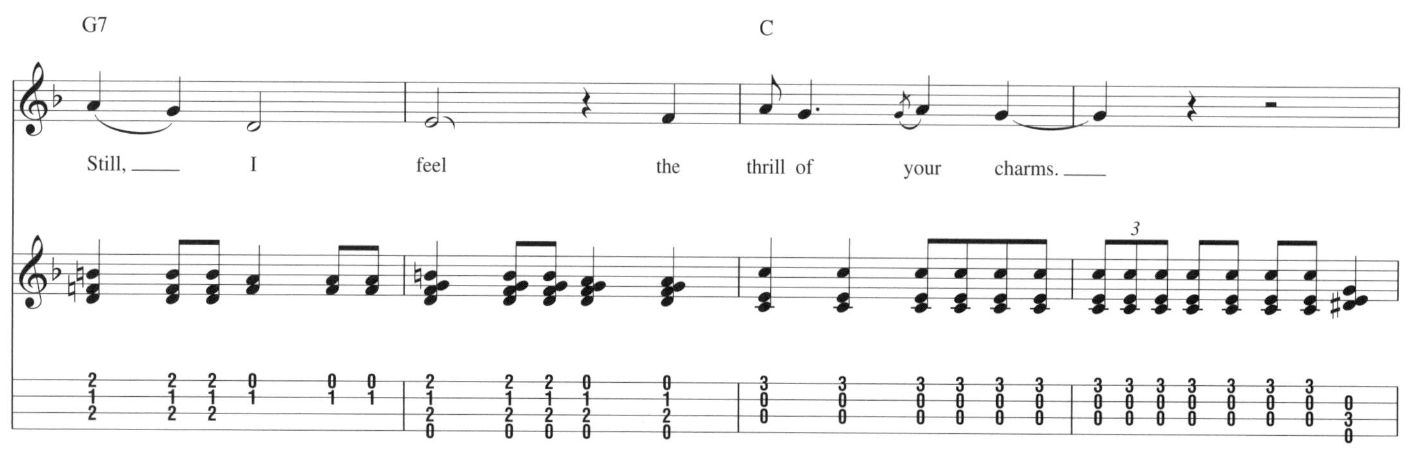
G7
C
Still, I feel the thrill of your charms.

Uke 1: w/ Rhy. Fig. 2
B♭
B♭m6
Lips that once were mine,
Uke 2

F
F6
C+
F6
ten - der eyes that shine.

Uke 2 tacet
Am7♭5
D7
D9
A
A7
Dm
F7
They will light my way to - night. I'll
Uke 1
Rhy. Fig. 3
B♭
B♭m6
C6
F
see you in my dreams. I'll
End Rhy. Fig. 3
Chorus
Uke 1: w/ Rhy. Fig. 2 (1st 4 meas.)
B♭
B♭m6
see you in my dreams,
F
C+
F6
hold you in my dreams.
Uke 1
D7
Some - one took you out of my arms.

G7
C7
Still, I feel the thrill of your charms.
Uke 1: w/ Rhy. Fig. 2
B♭
B♭m6
Lips that once were mine,
(Oo,
Uke 2
Uke 2 tacet
F
F6
C+
F6
Ten - der eyes that shine.
oo.)
Uke 1: w/ Rhy. Fig. 3
Am7♭5
D7
D9
A
A7
Dm
F7
They will light my way to - night. I'll
B♭
B♭m6
C6
see you in my
(See you in my

F
dreams.
dreams.)
Uke 1
Uke 2
Uke 1: w/ Rhy. Fig. 3
Uke 2 tacet
Am7♭5 D7 D9 A A7 Dm F7
They will light my lone - ly way to - night. I'll
B♭ B♭m6 C6
see you in my
(See you in my
Outro
F F6 Fmaj7 F6
dreams.
dreams.)
Uke 1
F F6 Fmaj7 F6 F
rit.

from Jake Shimabukuro - *My Life*

In My Life

Words and Music by John Lennon and Paul McCartney

Em
Em(maj7)
Em7
A7
Cm7
Cm6
G
D
D7
G
D
E
G
D/F♯
Em
G7
C
Cm
G
D/F♯
Em
G7
C
Cm7
G
Em
Em(maj7)
A7
F
G
Em
Em(maj7)
A7
Cm7
G
Cm7

F
G
Gadd9
G
D
G
D
Coda
Em
Em(maj7)
Em7
Am7
F
G
Em
Em(maj7)
A7
Cm7
Cm6
G
Cm7
Cm6
G
Cm7
Cm6
G
A tempo
G
D
G
D
Fmaj9(no3rd)
Gsus2(add♯4)
rit.

from Jake Shimabukuro - *Gently Weeps*

Misty

Music by Erroll Garner

Moderately slow ♩ = 88
Fmaj7
Cm9
F13♭9
B♭maj7
B♭m6
Fmaj7
Dm7
Gm7
C7
Fsus2
C7sus4
C
Fadd9
Cm7
F7♭9
B♭maj7
Bm11
E9
Am7
A♭7
Gm7
G♭7
D
Fmaj7
Harm.
Cm9
F13♭9
B♭maj9

Faster ♩ = 184
E
B♭m6
Fmaj7
D7♯9
Gm7
C7
F
C7sus4
Cm9
F9
F♯9
F13
B♭maj7
E♭9
Am7
Emaj7
F9sus4
D7♭9
F6

F
Cm7
F7♭9
B♭maj7
Bm11
E9
G6
Am7
A♭
Gm7
G♭7
G
F6/9
Cm9
F9sus4
F♯9
F13
B♭maj7
B♭m6
E♭7
3
Am7
D7♯9/13
D7♭9/♭13
D7♯9/13
Gm7
C7♯9/♯5
Am7
D7♭9
Gm7
C7♯9/♯5
Am7
D7♭9
Gm7
C7♯9/♯5
C7♭9/♯5
C7♯9/♯5
Am7
D7♯9/13
Gm7
C7♯9/♯5
Am7
A♭7
Gm7
G♭7
sf

Free time
N.C.
mp
mf
H
Fmaj7
Cm9
F13♭9
B♭maj7
B♭m6
Fmaj7
D7♯9
Gm7
C7♭9
Am7
D7♭9
Gm7
G♭maj7
F
C13♭9
Fadd9
Fmaj13
mp

from Various Artists (Moe Keale) - *Legends of the Ukulele, Vol. 2*

Moonglow

Words and Music by Will Hudson, Eddie De Lange and Irving Mills

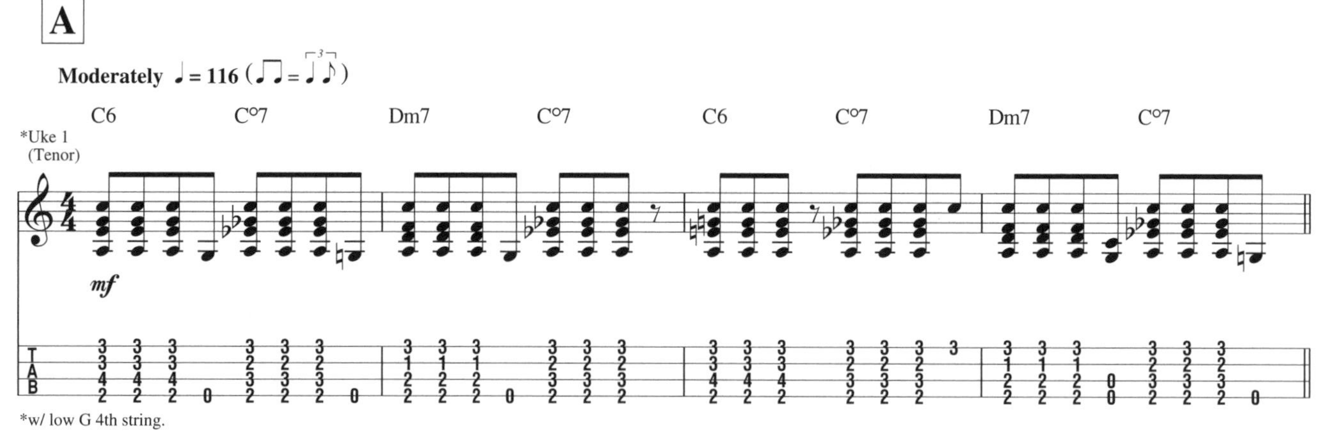

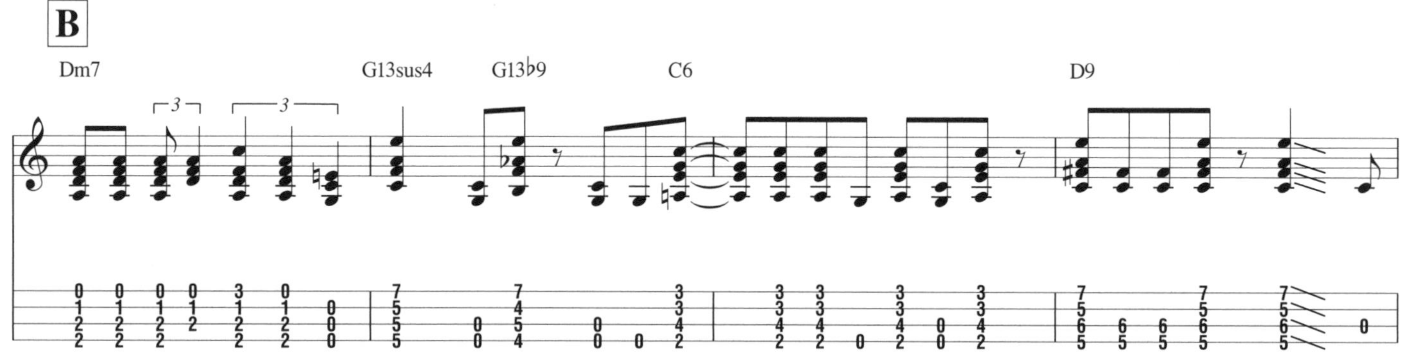

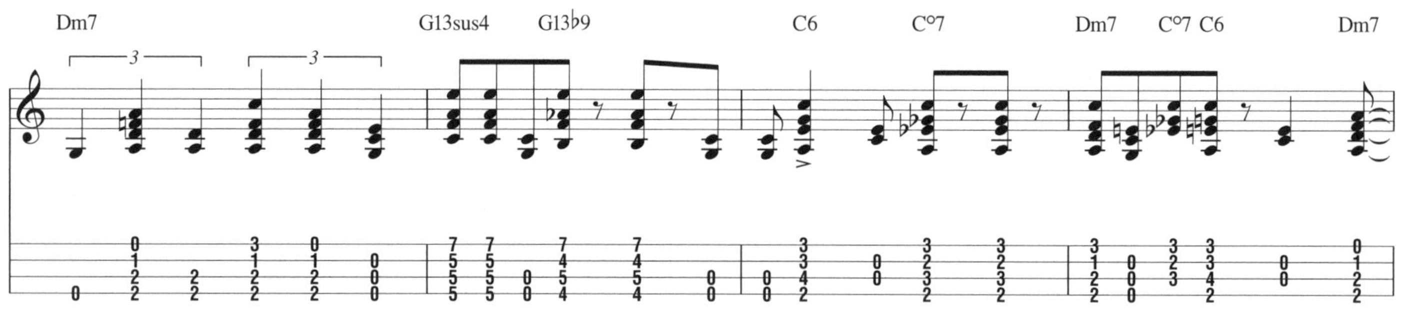

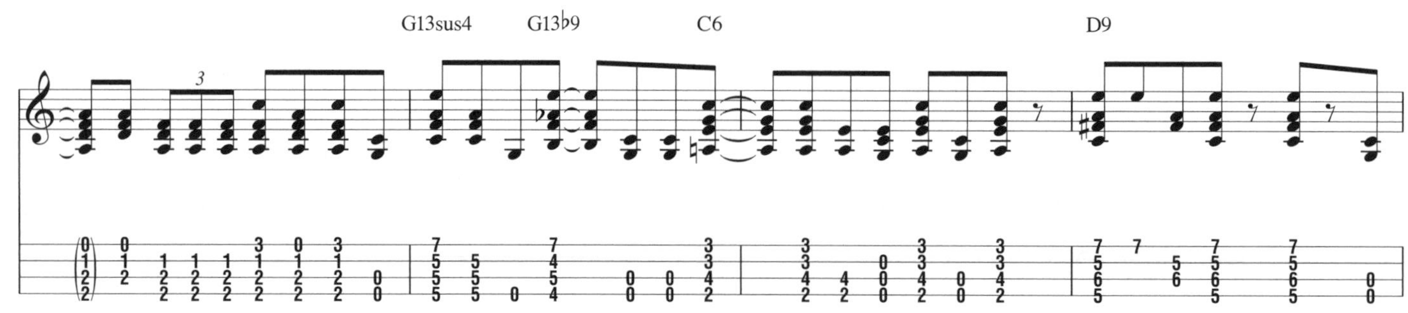

Dm7
G13sus4
G13♭9
C6
C°7
Dm7
C°7 C6
C
C9
B9
B♭9
A9
D9
G7
A♭9
G7
Dm7
D
Dm7
G13sus4
G13♭9
C6
D9
Dm7
G13sus4
G13♭9
C6
C°7
Dm7
C°7 C6
B♭9
B9
C9

E
C9
B9
B♭9
A9
A13
D9
G7
A♭9
G7
G♭
Dm7
F
Dm7
G13sus4
G13♭9
C6
D9
Dm7
G13sus4
G13♭9
C6
C°7
Dm7
C°7
C6
C°7
Dm7
C°7
C6
C°7
Dm7
C°7
C6
Harm.

from Israel "IZ" Kamakawiwo'ole - *Facing Future*

Over the Rainbow/ What a Wonderful World

Over the Rainbow
from THE WIZARD OF OZ
Music by Harold Arlen
Lyric by E.Y. "Yip" Harburg

What a Wonderful World
Words and Music by George David Weiss and Bob Thiele

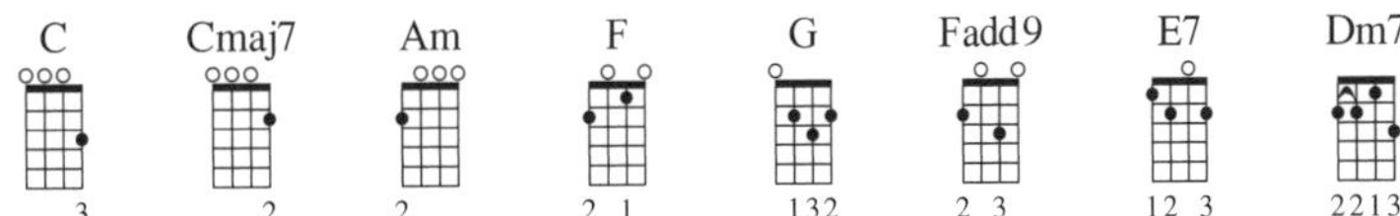

Tenor ukulele tuning:
(low to high) G-C-E-A

Spoken: 'Kay, this one's for Gabby.

Intro
Moderately ♩ = 85

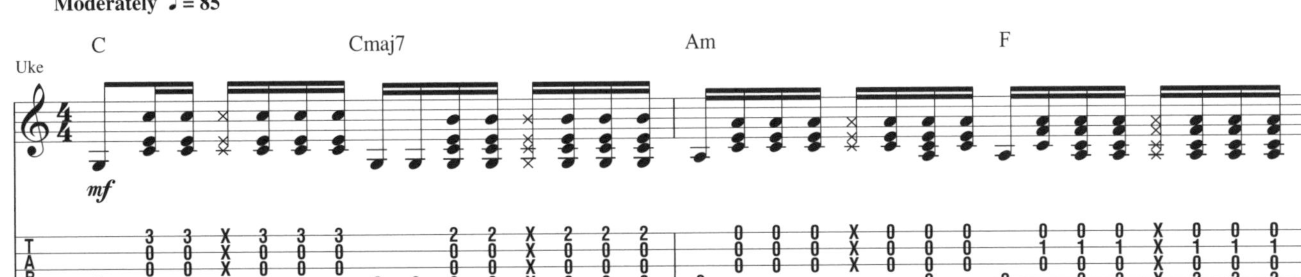

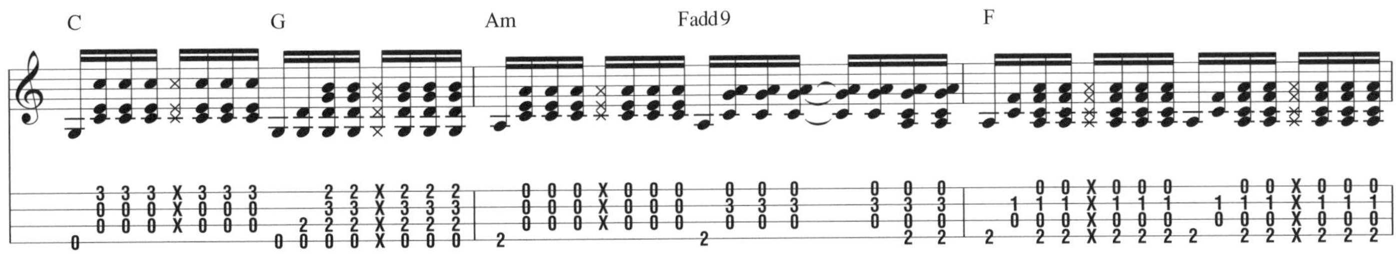

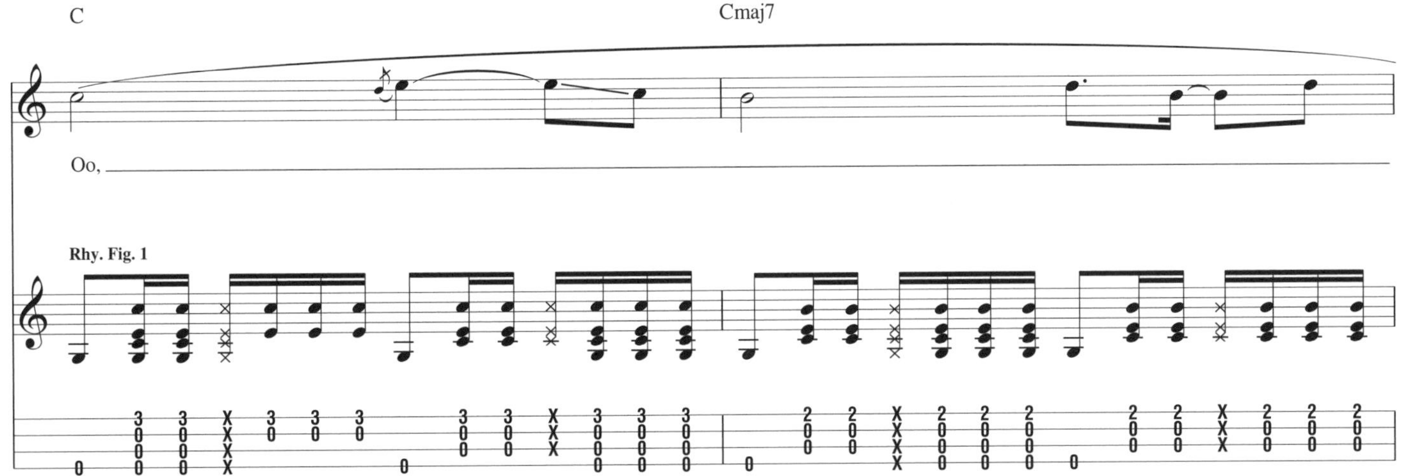

F
C
oo, hoo, hoo.
End Rhy. Fig. 1
F
E7
Oo,
Rhy. Fig. 2
End Rhy. Fig. 2
Am
F
oo, hoo, hoo, hoo, hoo, hoo.
Verse
Uke: w/ Rhy. Fig. 1
C
Cmaj7
F
C
1. Some - where o - ver the rain - bow, way up high,

F
C
and the dreams that you dream of
Uke
Rhy. Fig. 3

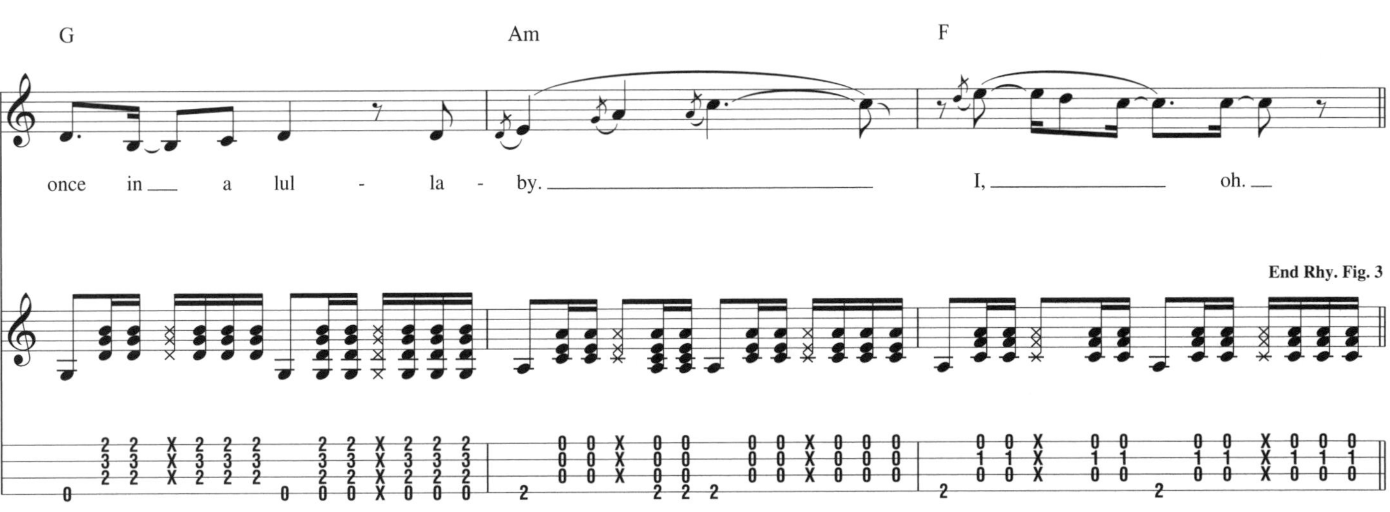
G
Am
F
once in a lul - la - by.
I, oh.
End Rhy. Fig. 3

Verse

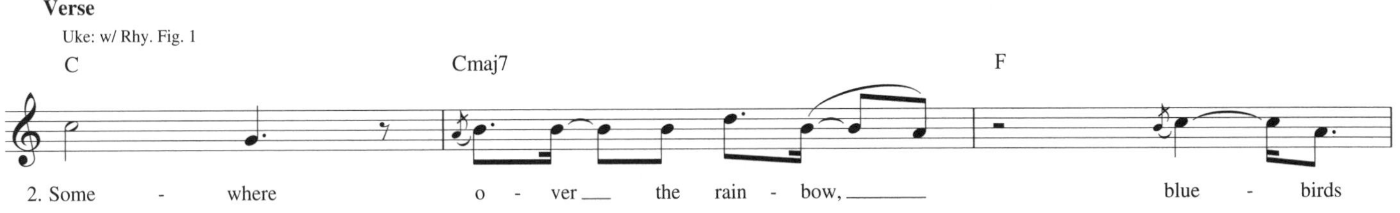
Uke: w/ Rhy. Fig. 1
C
Cmaj7
F
2. Some - where o - ver the rain - bow,
blue - birds

Uke: w/ Rhy. Fig. 3
C
F
C
fly.
And the dreams that you dream of,

G
Am
F
dreams real - ly do come true,
oo.
Some -

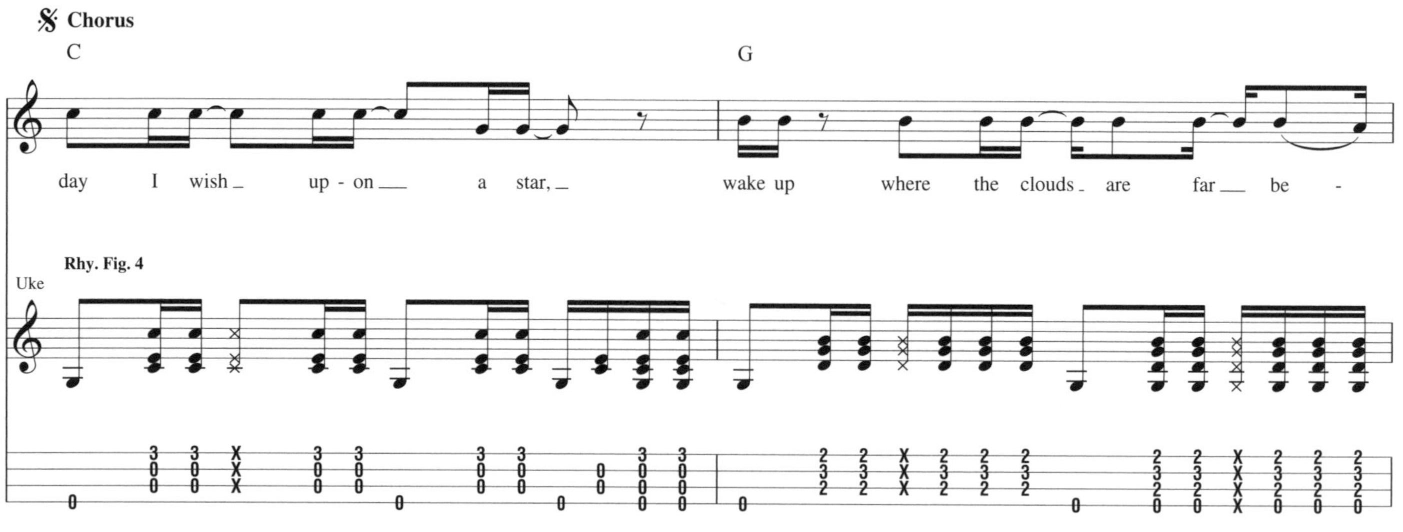
Chorus
C
G
day I wish up - on a star,
wake up where the clouds are far be -
Rhy. Fig. 4
Uke

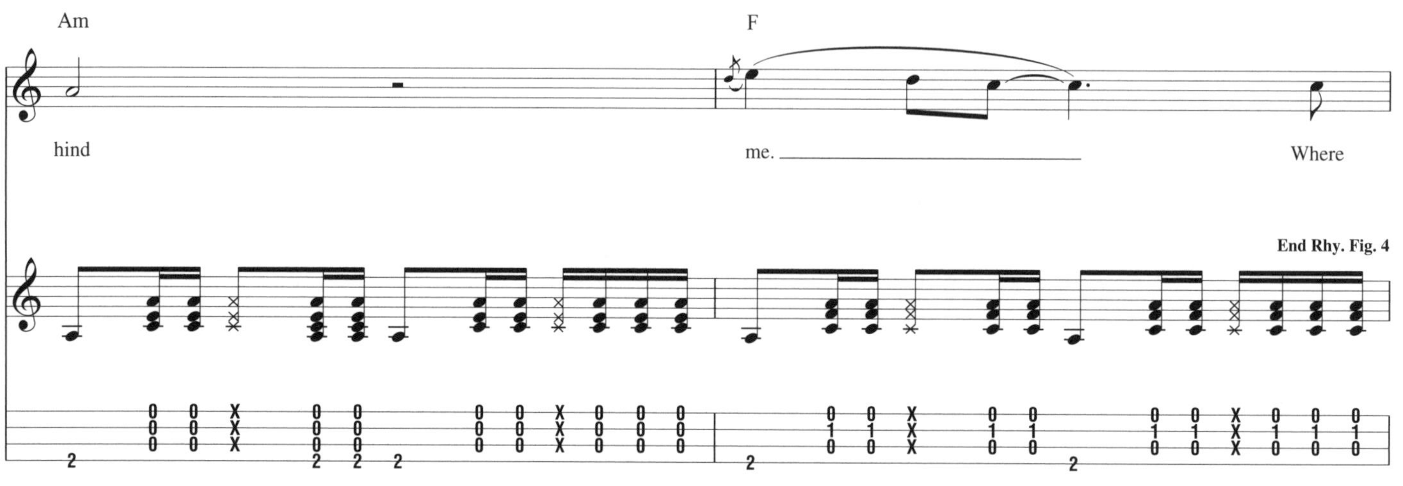
Am
F
hind
me.
Where
End Rhy. Fig. 4

Uke: w/ Rhy. Fig. 4
C
G
Am
trou-ble melts like lem-on drops,
high a - bove the chim - a - ney top, that's where
you'll

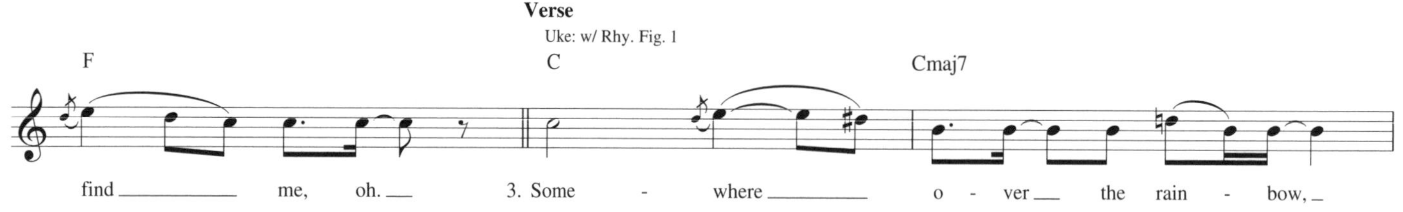
Verse
Uke: w/ Rhy. Fig. 1
F
C
Cmaj7
find me, oh.
3. Some - where
o - ver the rain - bow,

Uke: w/ Rhy. Fig. 3
F
C
F
C
blue - birds fly.
way up high.
And the
dreams that you dare to. Oh

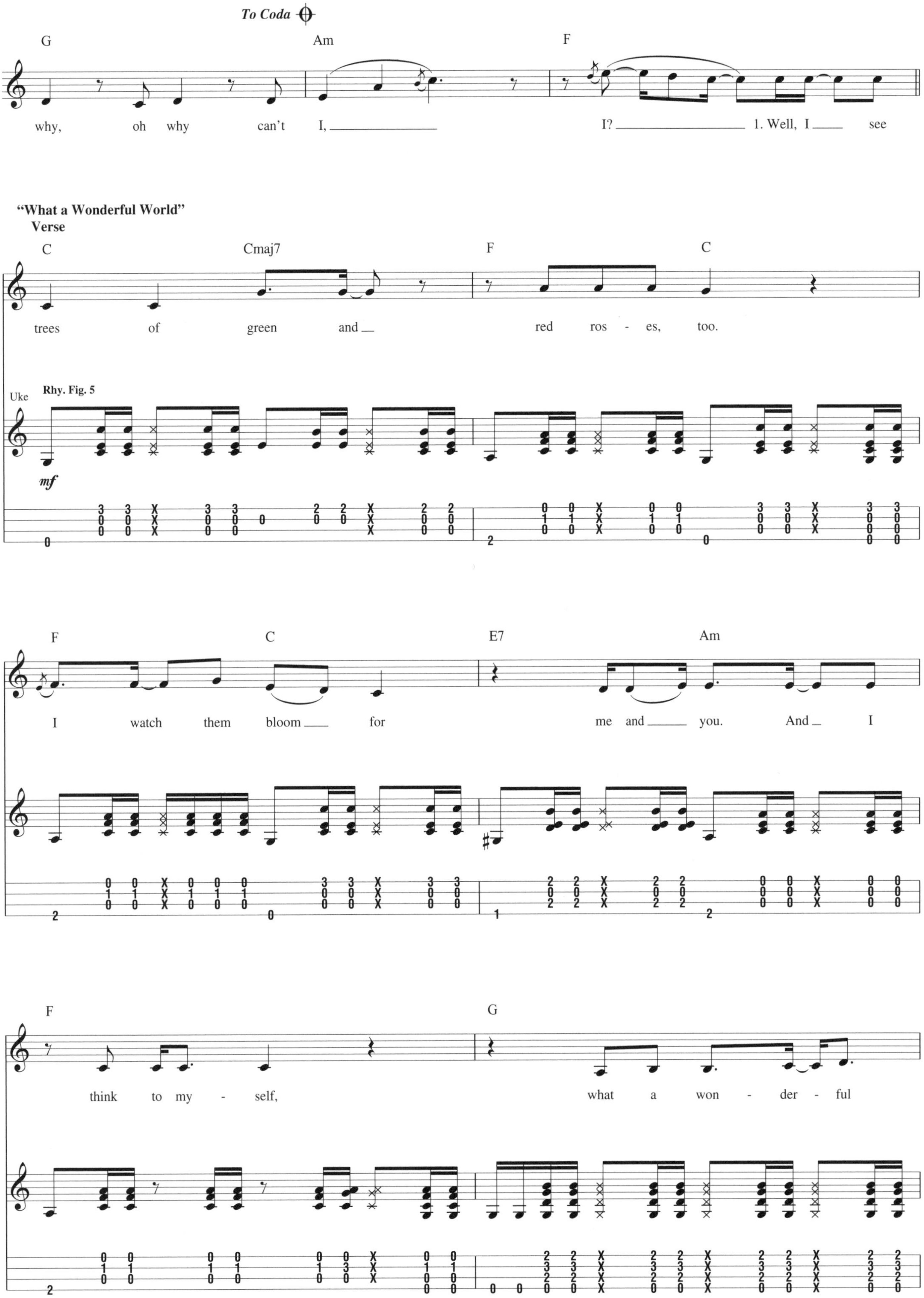

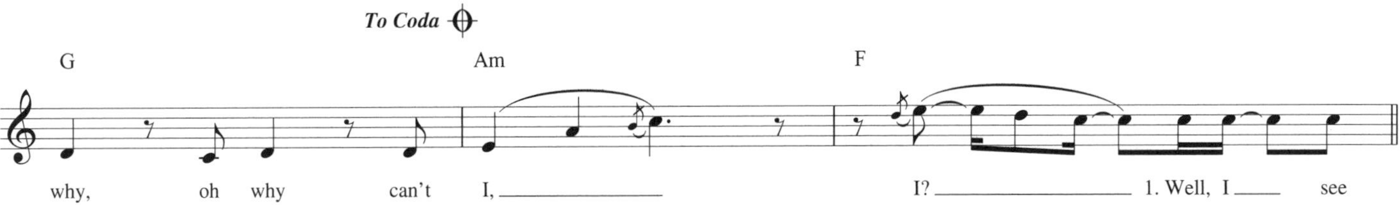

"What a Wonderful World"
Verse

C Cmaj7 F C

trees of green and red ros - es, too.

Uke

Rhy. Fig. 5

mf

F C E7 Am

I watch them bloom for me and you. And I

F G

think to my - self, what a won - der - ful

Verse

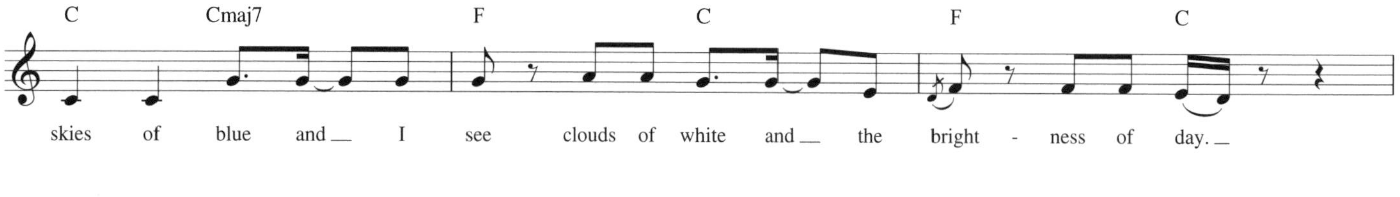

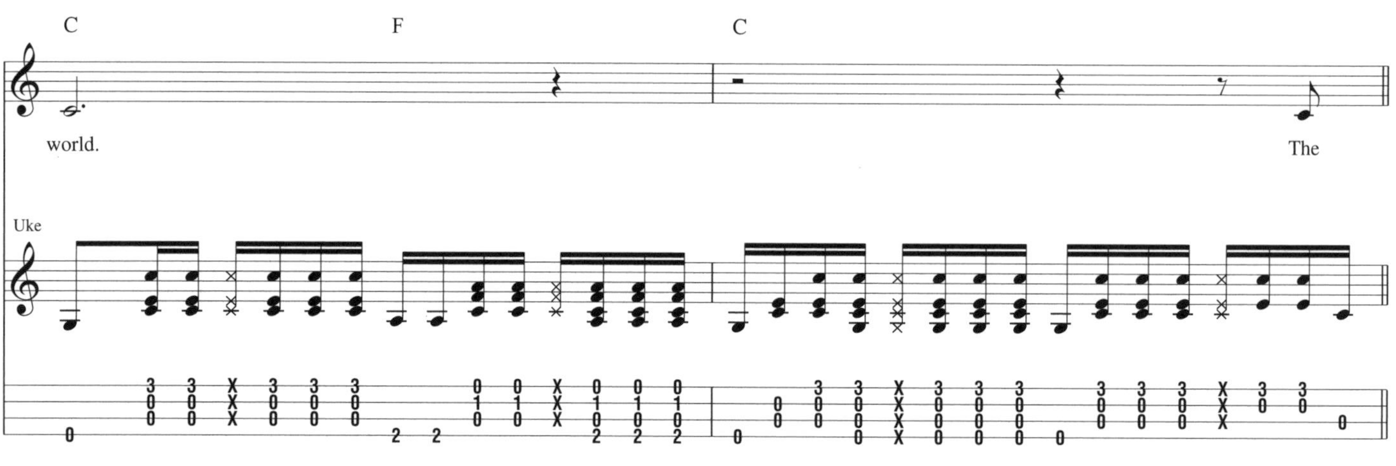

Chorus

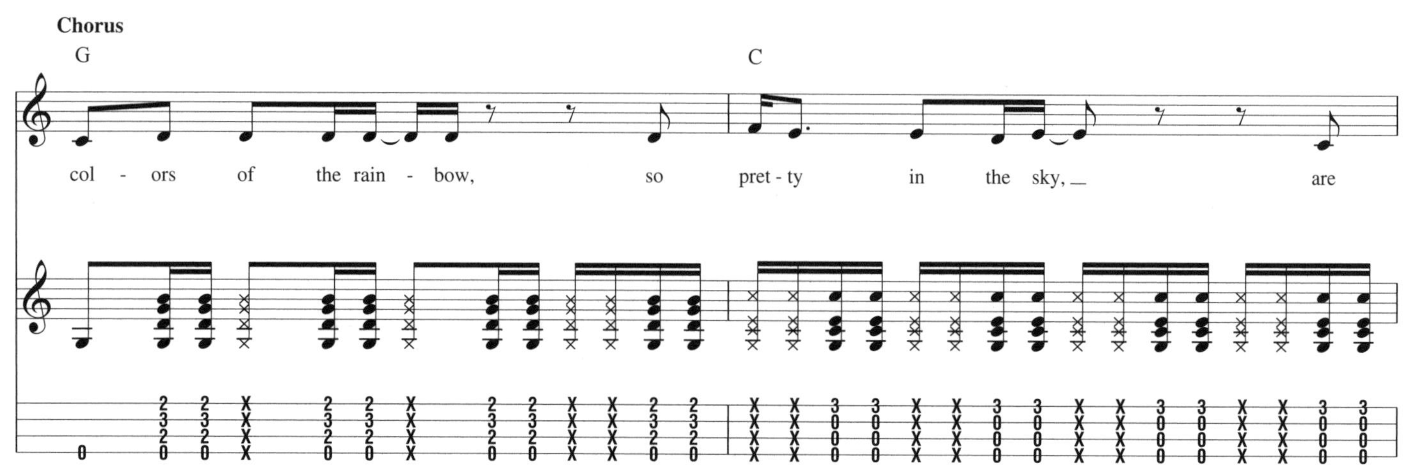

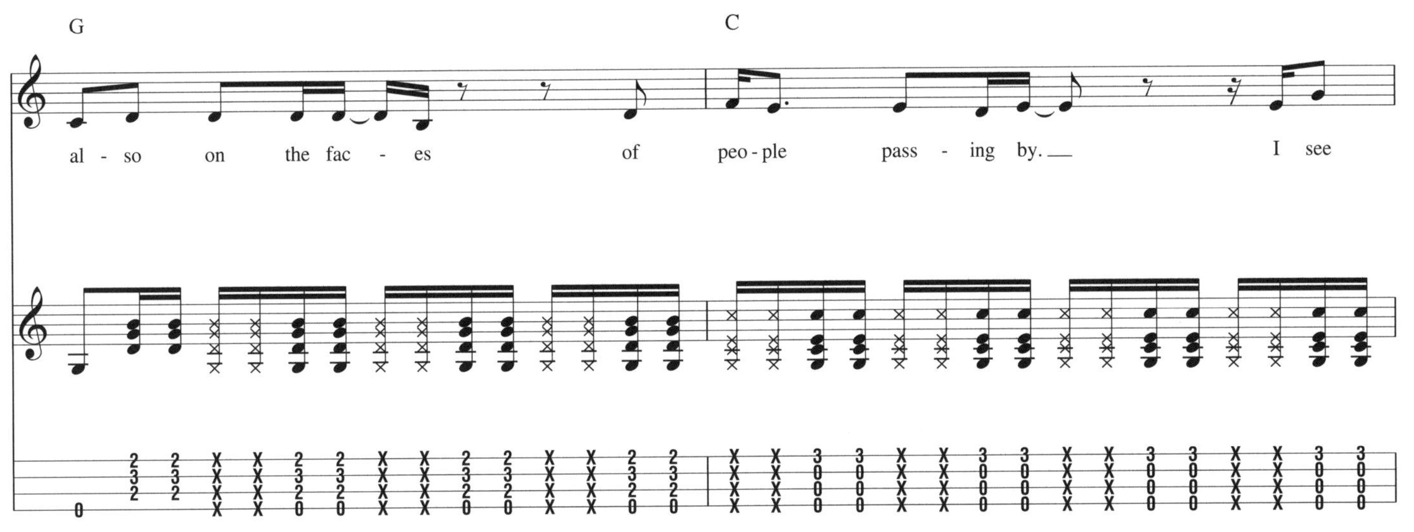
G
C
al - so on the fac - es of peo - ple pass - ing by.
I see

F
C
F
C
friends shak - in' hands, say - in', "How do you do?"

F
C
Dm7
G
They're real - ly say - in', "I, I love you."
3. I hear

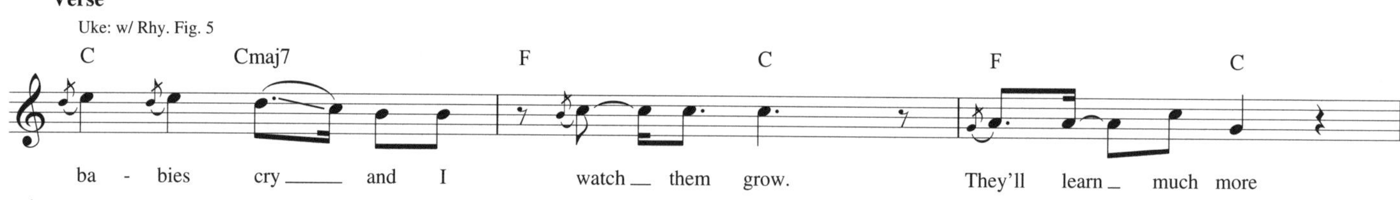
Verse
Uke: w/ Rhy. Fig. 5
C Cmaj7 F C F C
ba - bies cry ___ and I watch __ them grow. They'll learn __ much more

E7 Am F G
than we'll __ know. And __ I think to my - self, what a won - der - ful

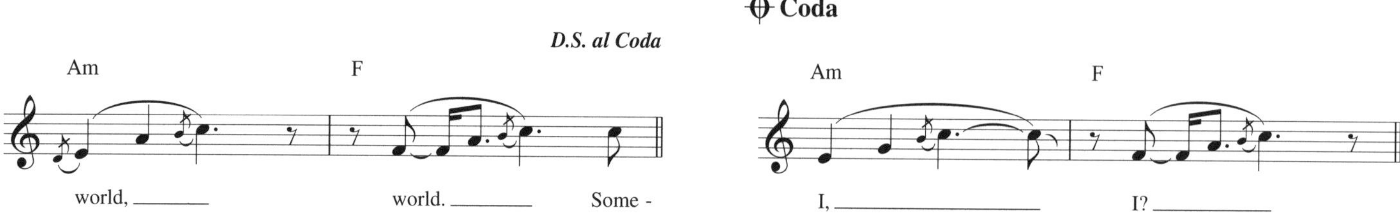
Coda
D.S. al Coda
Am F Am F
world, ___ world. ___ Some - I, ___ I? ___

Outro
Uke: w/ Rhy. Fig. 1
C Cmaj7 F
Oo, ___ oo,

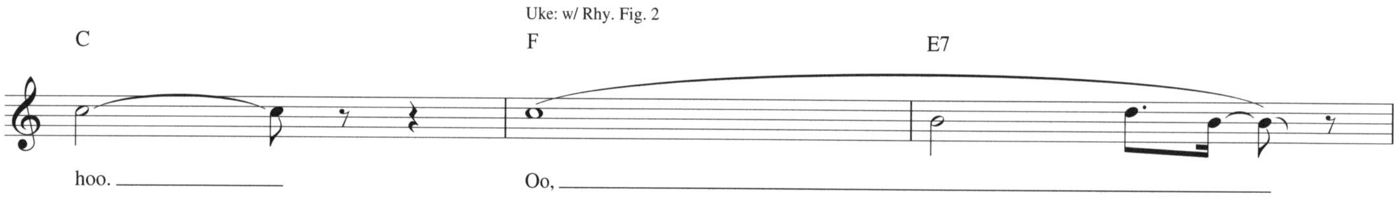
Uke: w/ Rhy. Fig. 2
C F E7
hoo. ___ Oo, ___

Begin fade
Fade out
Am F C
Oo, ah, ah, eh, __ ah, ah, ah, ah, ah, ah, ah, ah, ah, ah.
Uke

from The Kalima Brothers & The Richard Kauhi Quartette - *The Kalima Brothers & The Richard Kauhi Quartet*

Stars and Stripes Forever

By John Philip Sousa

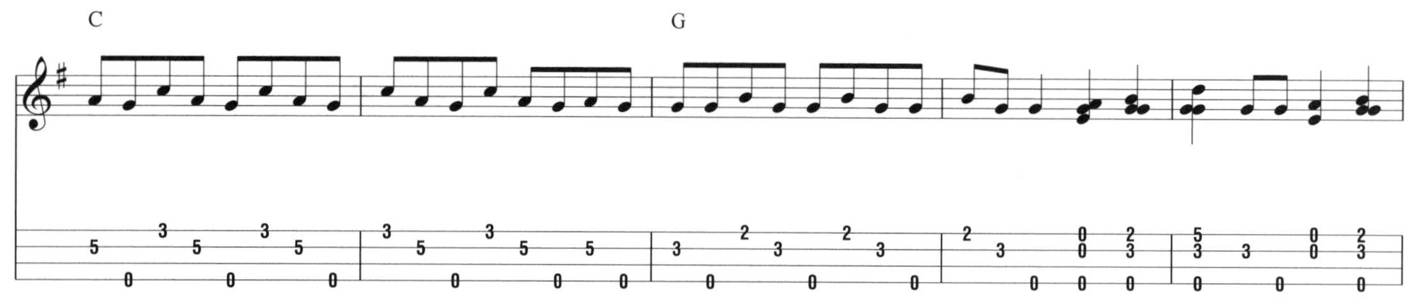

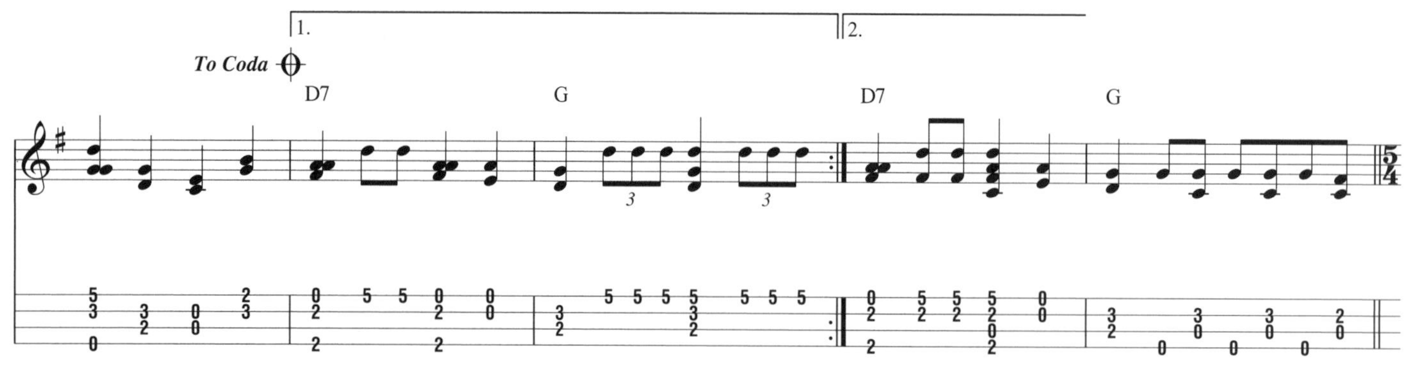

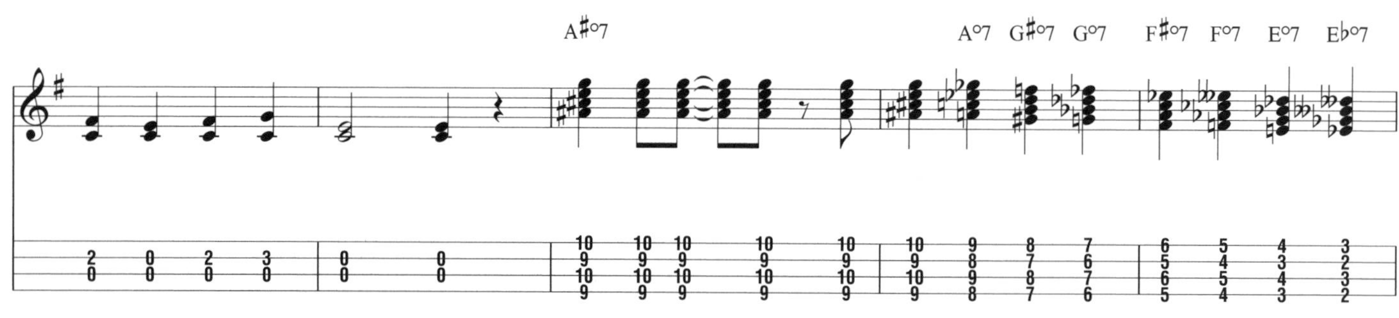

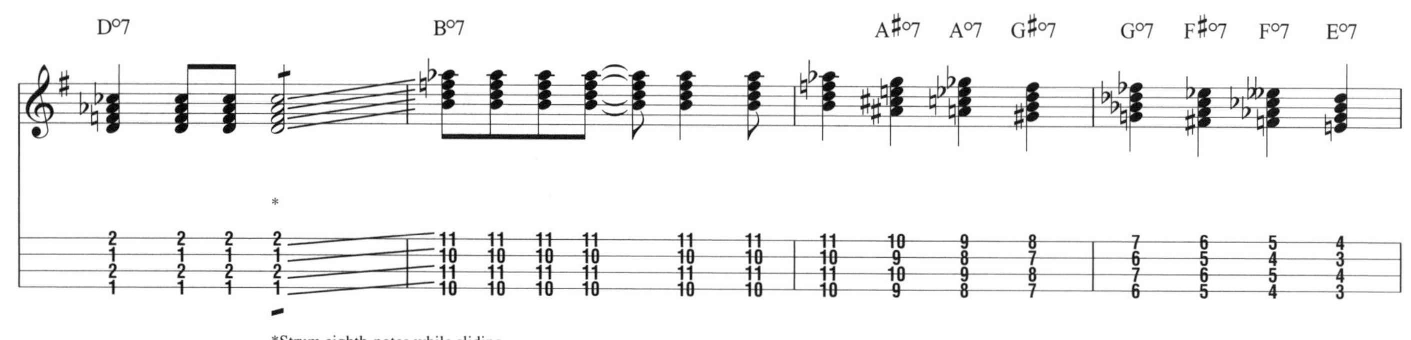

*Strum eighth-notes while sliding.

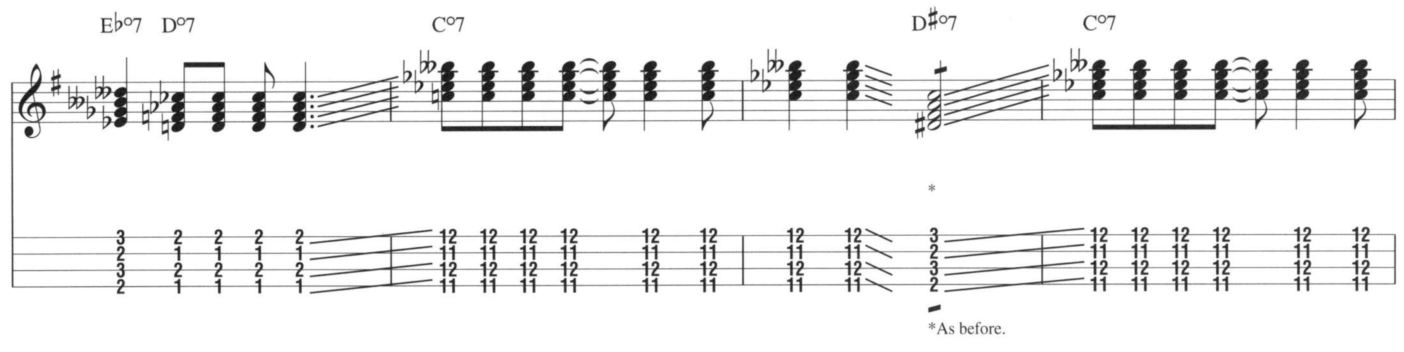
E♭°7
D°7
C°7
D♯°7
C°7
*
*As before.

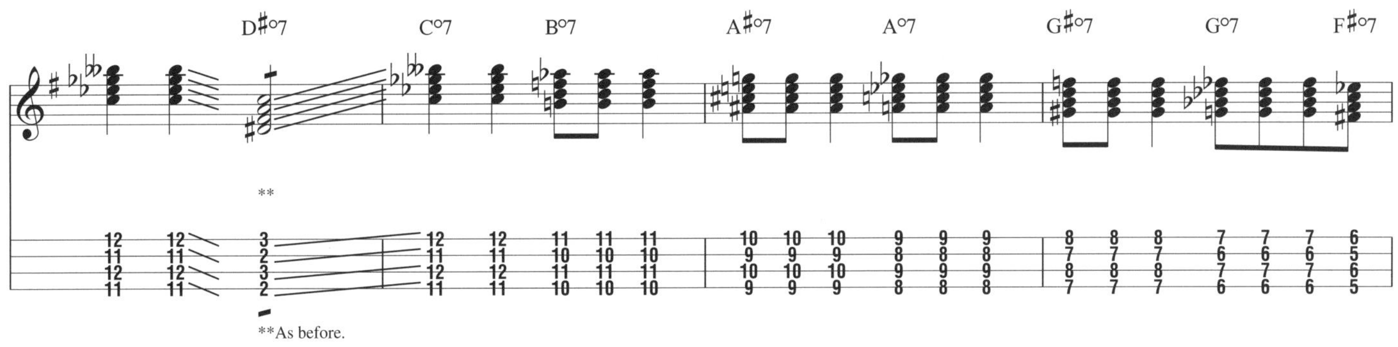
D♯°7
C°7
B°7
A♯°7
A°7
G♯°7
G°7
F♯°7
**
**As before.

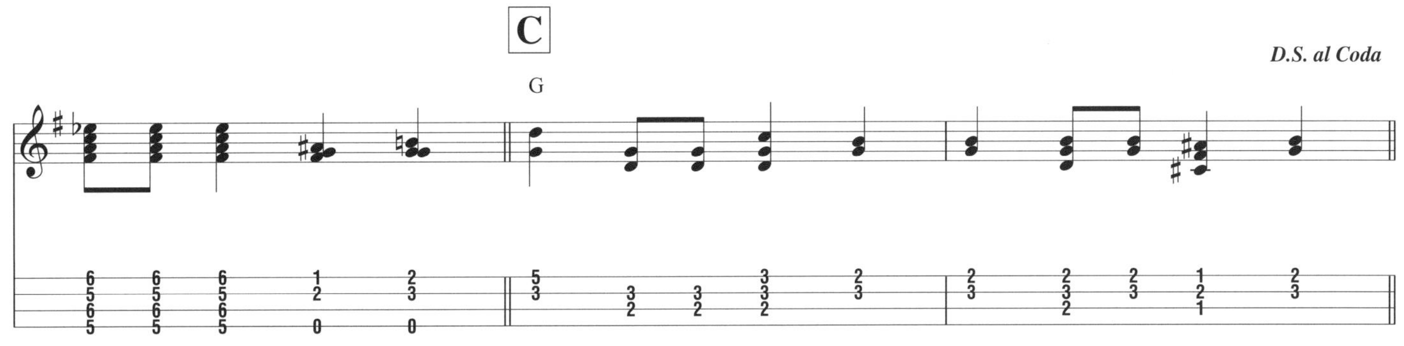
C
D.S. al Coda
G

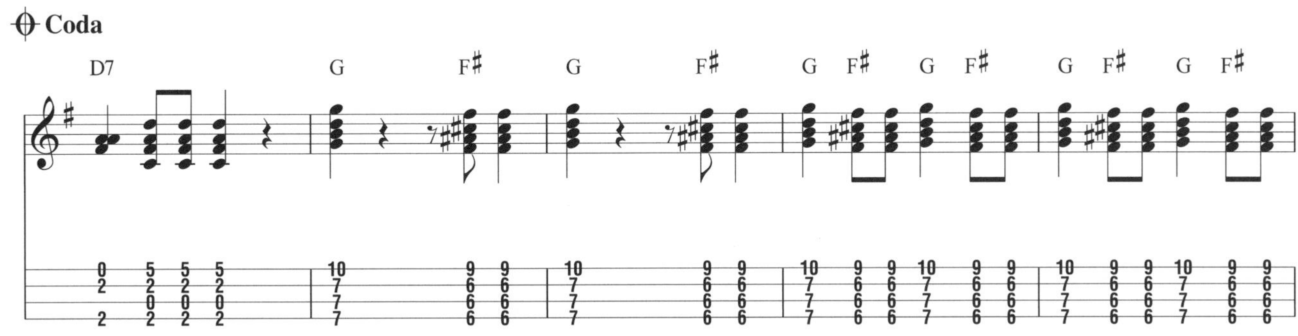
Coda
D7
G
F♯
G
F♯
G
F♯
G
F♯
G
F♯
G
F♯

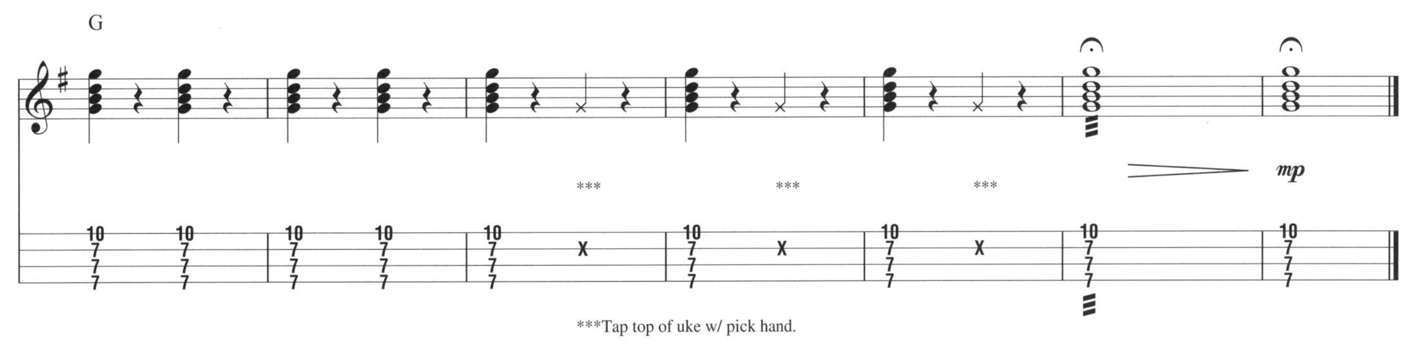
G
***
***
***
mp
***Tap top of uke w/ pick hand.

from Various Artists (Roy Smeck) - *With My Little Ukulele in My Hand*

Tiger Rag
(Hold That Tiger)

Words by Harry DeCosta
Music by Original Dixieland Jazz Band

Tenor Banjo tuning (low to high): C-G-D-A

*Tenor Banjo arr. for Tenor Uke, w/ low G 4th string.

C7
F
C7
F
C7
F
C7
F
C
B♭
C7
F
C7
F

C7
F
C7
F
D
B♭
F7
B♭
F7
B♭
E
E♭
N.C.
E♭
N.C.
E♭
N.C.
B♭7
N.C.
B♭7
E♭
F7
B♭7
N.C.
B♭7

E♭
B♭7
E♭
N.C.
B♭7
E♭
A♭
E♭7
A♭
B7
B♭7
E♭
E♭7
F
A♭
E♭7

A♭
N.C.
A♭
A♭7
D♭
8va
loco
A♭°7
A♭
F7
B♭7
E♭7
A♭
N.C.
8va
G
N.C.
8va
8va
E♭7

Ab N.C.
8va
Ab
8va
loco
Ab7 Db Ab°7
8va
Ab F7 Bb7 Eb7
8va
H
Ab N.C. Ab
8va
Eb7
8va

8va
A♭
N.C.
A♭
A♭7
D♭
A♭°7
A♭
F7
B♭7
E♭7
A♭
N.C.
loco
I
A♭
loco

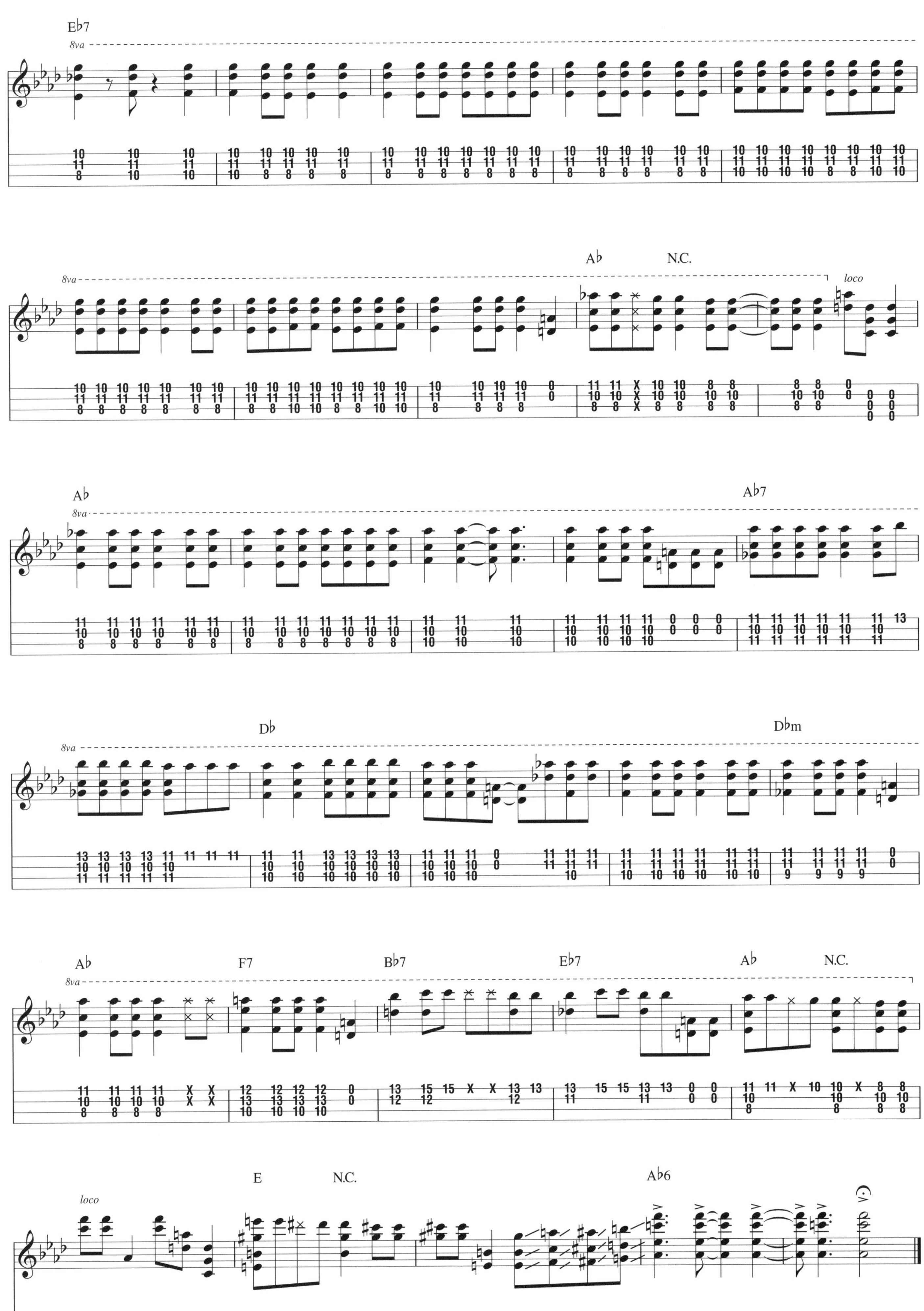
E♭7
8va
8va
A♭
N.C.
loco
A♭
8va
A♭7
8va
D♭
D♭m
A♭
F7
B♭7
E♭7
A♭
N.C.
8va
loco
E
N.C.
A♭6

from Tiny Tim - *God Bless Tiny Tim*

Tip-Toe Thru' the Tulips With Me

Words by Al Dubin
Music by Joe Burke

E A E E7
me.
Uke
Rhy. Fig. 2
End Rhy. Fig. 2
Bridge
A G♯m C♯7
Knee deep in flow - ers we'll stray.
G♯m F♯7 B7
We'll keep the show - ers a - way. 3., 4. And if I
Verse
Uke: w/ Rhy. Fig. 1
E B7 E E7
kiss you in the gar - den, in the moon - light, will you
To Coda
A Am E B7
par - don me? And tip - toe through the tu - lips with

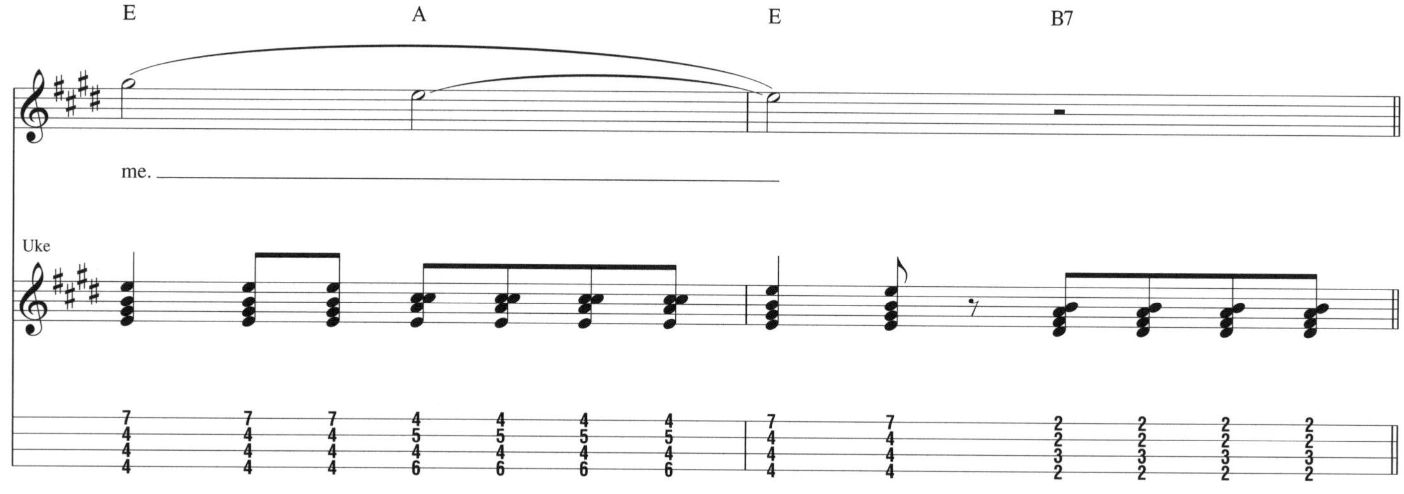

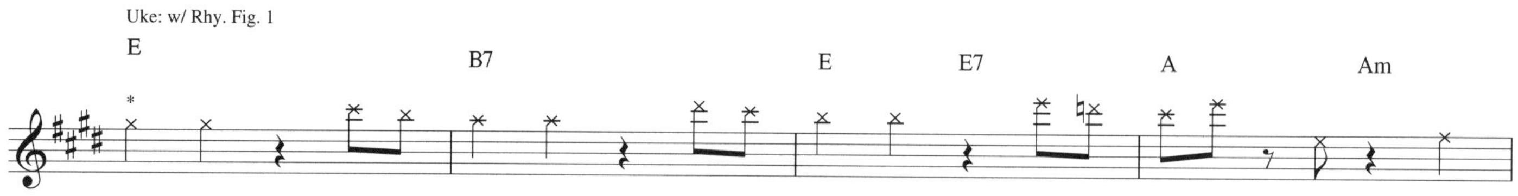

*Click with tongue & roof of mouth.

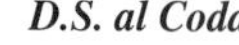

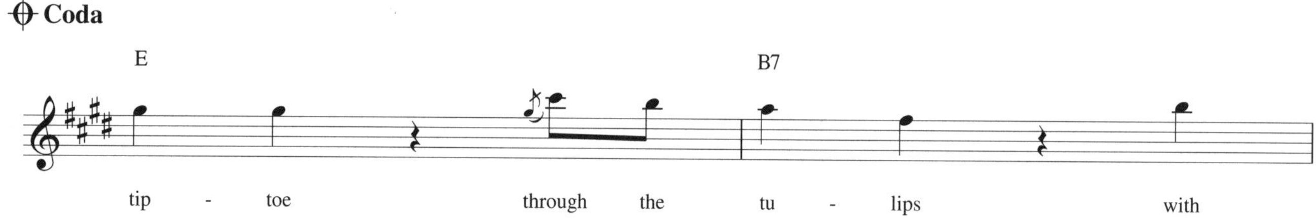

from Roy Smeck - *The Magic Ukulele of Roy Smeck*

Twelfth Street Rag

By Euday L. Bowman

Tune up 1 step:
(low to high) A-D-F♯-B

C6
G7
C6
C
Cadd9
C7
C Cadd9
F
C°7
C
D7
G7
C
G7
C
C
G°7
G7
G°7
G7
G°7
G7
D
C6
G7

C6
G7
D7
G7
C6
G7
C6
C
C7
F
A♭7

C
D7
G7
C
G7
C
G7
C
E
G7
G°7
G7
F
C6
G7
C6
G7
D7
1/4
1/4
1/4
G7

C6
G7
C6
C7
F
A♭7
1/2
1/2
D7
G7
C6
G7
C
G
G°7
G7
G°7
G7
G°7
G7
G°7
G7
H
C
G7

C
G7
D7
G7
C6
G7
C6
C
C7
F
F♯°7
C
D7
G7
C
C7
D7
Fm
C
G7
C
C6
*Flutter body of uke.

from George Formby - *When I'm Cleaning Windows - His 52 Finest 1936-1946*

When I'm Cleaning Windows

Words and Music by Fred Cliffe, George Formby and Harry Gifford

Tune down 1 step:
(low to high) F-B♭-D-G

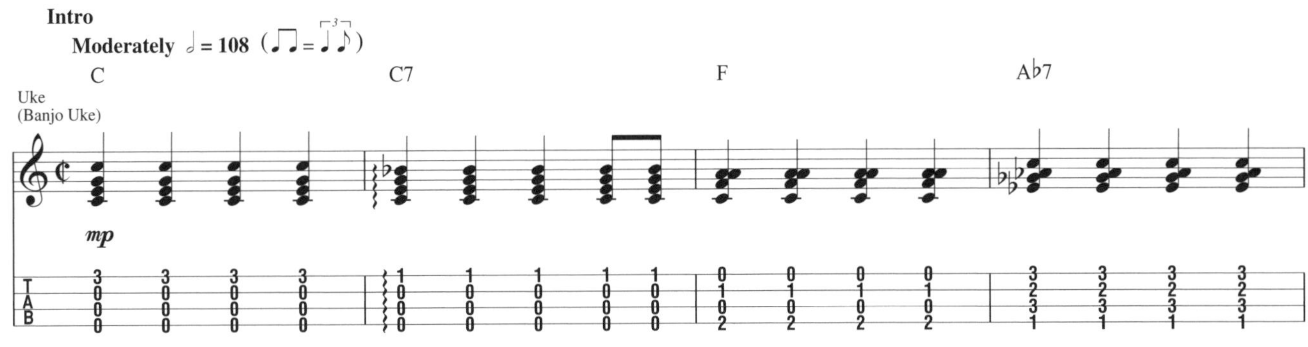

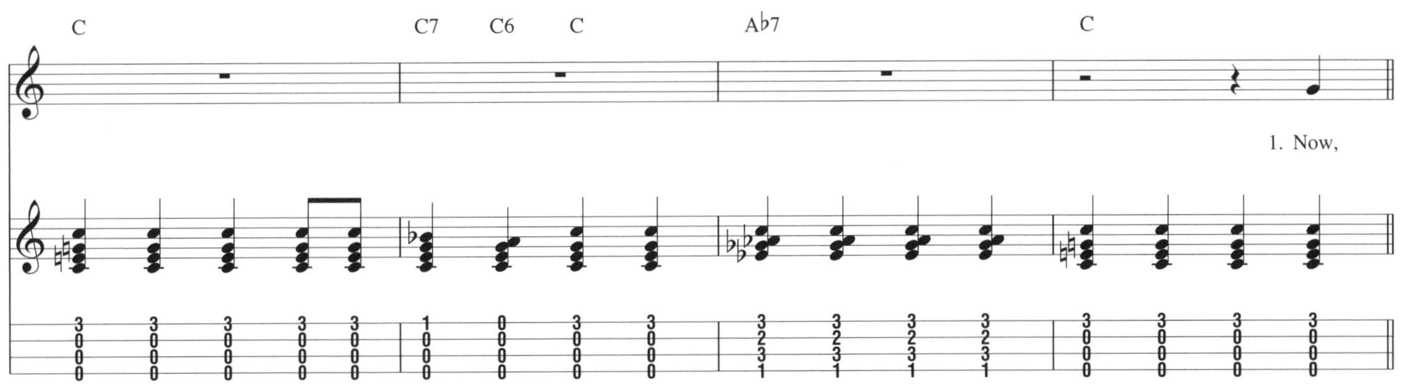

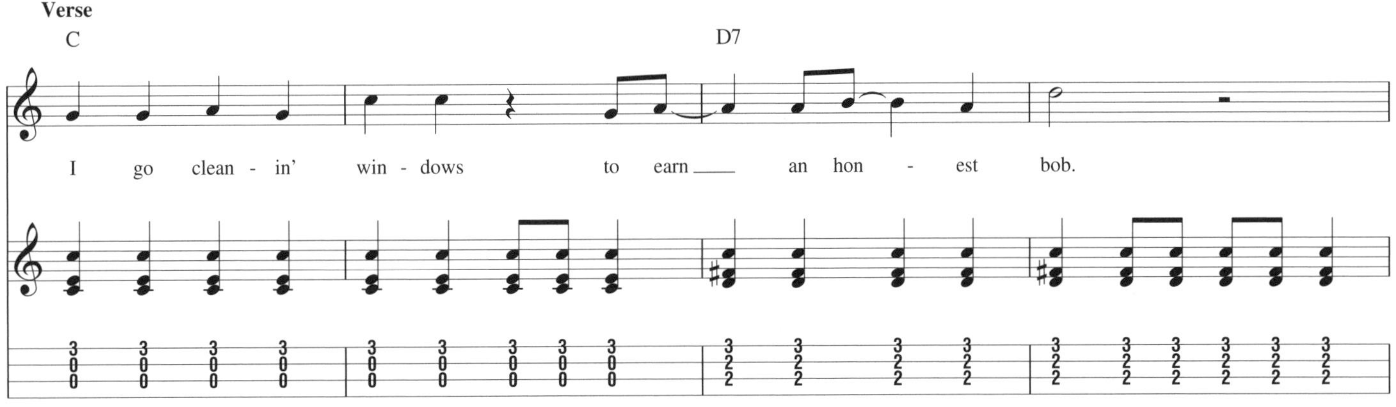

Verse
C C7 F A♭7
it's a job that just suits me. A win - dow clean - er you would be if
cham - ber - maid, sweet names I call. It's a won - der I don't fall. My
Rhy. Fig. 1
C C7 C6 C A♭7 C
you can see what I can see when I'm clean - in' win - dows.
mind's not on my work at all when I'm clean - in' win - dows. 6. I
End Rhy. Fig. 1
Verse
Uke: w/ Rhy. Fig. 1
C C7 F A♭7
3. Hon - ey - moon - in' coup - les, too. You should see them bill and coo. You'd
know a fel - la, such a swell. He has a thirst; that's plain to tell. I've
C C7 C6 C A♭7 C
be sur - prised at things they do when I'm clean - in' win - dows. In
seen him drink his bath as well when I'm clean - in' win - dows. Oh, in
Bridge
E7 A7
my pro - fes - sion I'll work hard, but I'll nev - er stop. I'll
Uke
Rhy. Fig. 2

D7
G7
climb this blink - in' lad - der 'til I get right to the top.
4. The
7. Pa -
End Rhy. Fig. 2
Verse
Uke: w/ Rhy. Fig. 1
C
C7
F
blush - in' bride, she looks di - vine. The bride - groom, he is
jam - as ly - in' side by side, lad - ies' night - ies I
A♭7
C
C7
C6
C
do - in' fine. I'd rath - er have his job than mine
have spied. I've of - ten seen what goes in - side.
1.
2.
when I'm clean - in' win - dows. 5. The
when I'm clean - in' win - dows.
Banjo Uke Solo
Uke

C
C7
C6
C
A♭7
C
E7
A7
D7
G7
C
C7
F
A♭7
C
C7
C6
C
A♭7
C6
8. Now,
Verse
Uke: w/ Rhy. Fig. 1
C
C7
F
A♭7
there's a fam - ous talk - ie queen; she looks a flap - per on the screen. She's
C
C7
C6
C
A♭7
C
more like eigh - ty than eight - een, when I'm clean - in' win - dows. 9. She

Verse
Uke: w/ Rhy. Fig. 1
C C7 F A♭7
pulls her hair all down be - hind, then pulls down her nev - er - mind. And
C C7 C6 C A♭7 C
af - ter that pulls down the blind, when I'm clean - in' win - dows. In
Bridge
Uke: w/ Rhy. Fig. 2
E7 A7
my pro - fes - sion I'll work hard, but I'll nev - er stop. I'll
D7 G7
climb this blink - in' lad - der 'til I get right to the top. 10. An old
Verse
Uke: w/ Rhy. Fig. 1
C C7 F A♭7
maid walks a - round the floor. She's so fed up, one day, I'm sure, she'll
C C7 C6 C A♭7 C
drag me in and lock the door when I'm clean - in' win - dows.
Outro
Uke: w/ Rhy. Fig. 1 (1st 6 meas.)
C C7 F A♭7 C C7 C6 C
A♭7 C N.C.
When I'm clean - in' win - dows.
Uke

from Andy Eastwood - *Ukulele Mania*

William Tell Overture

By G. Rossini

Tune up 2 steps:
(low to high) B-E-G♯-C♯

*Chord symbols reflect implied harmony.

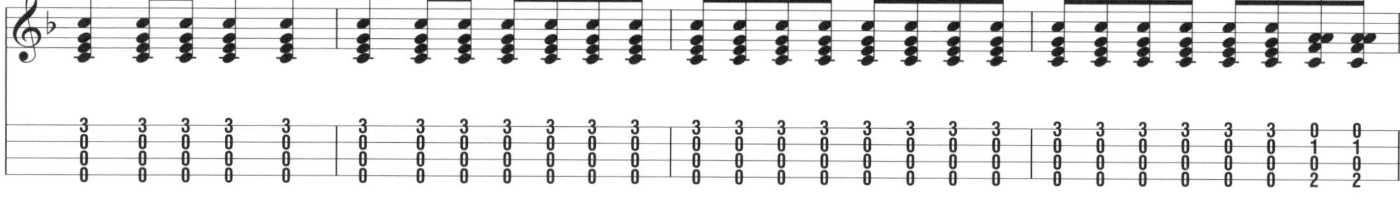

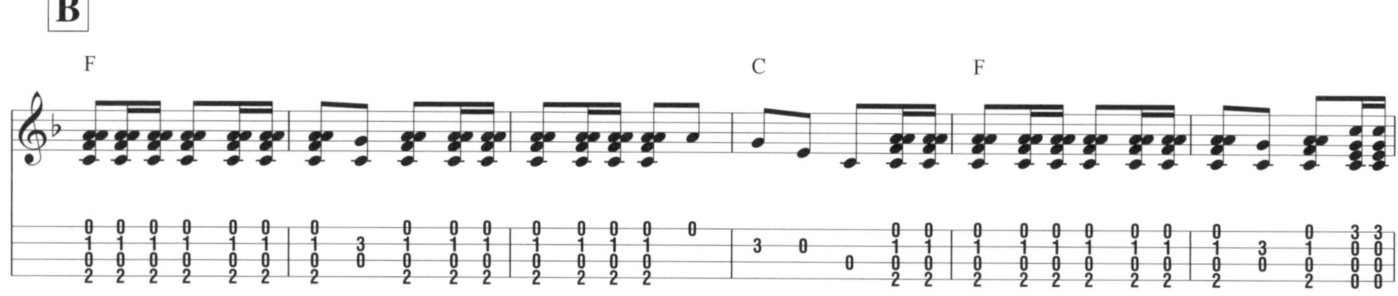

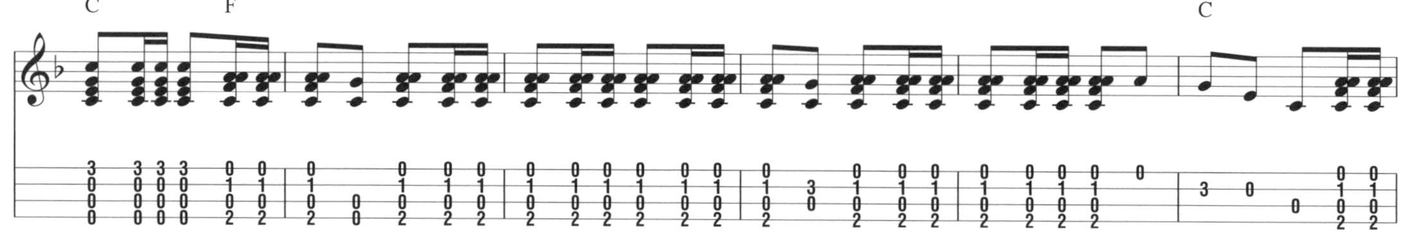

F
C
F
C
Dm
G7
C
G7
C
G7
C
Dm
G7
C
G7
C
G7
C
C7
F
C
C7
F
C
C7
F

C
G7
C
G7
C
G7
C
D
F
C
F
C
F
C
F
C
F
To Coda 2
E
F
A7
B♭
F
B♭
F
G7
C7
F
A7
3

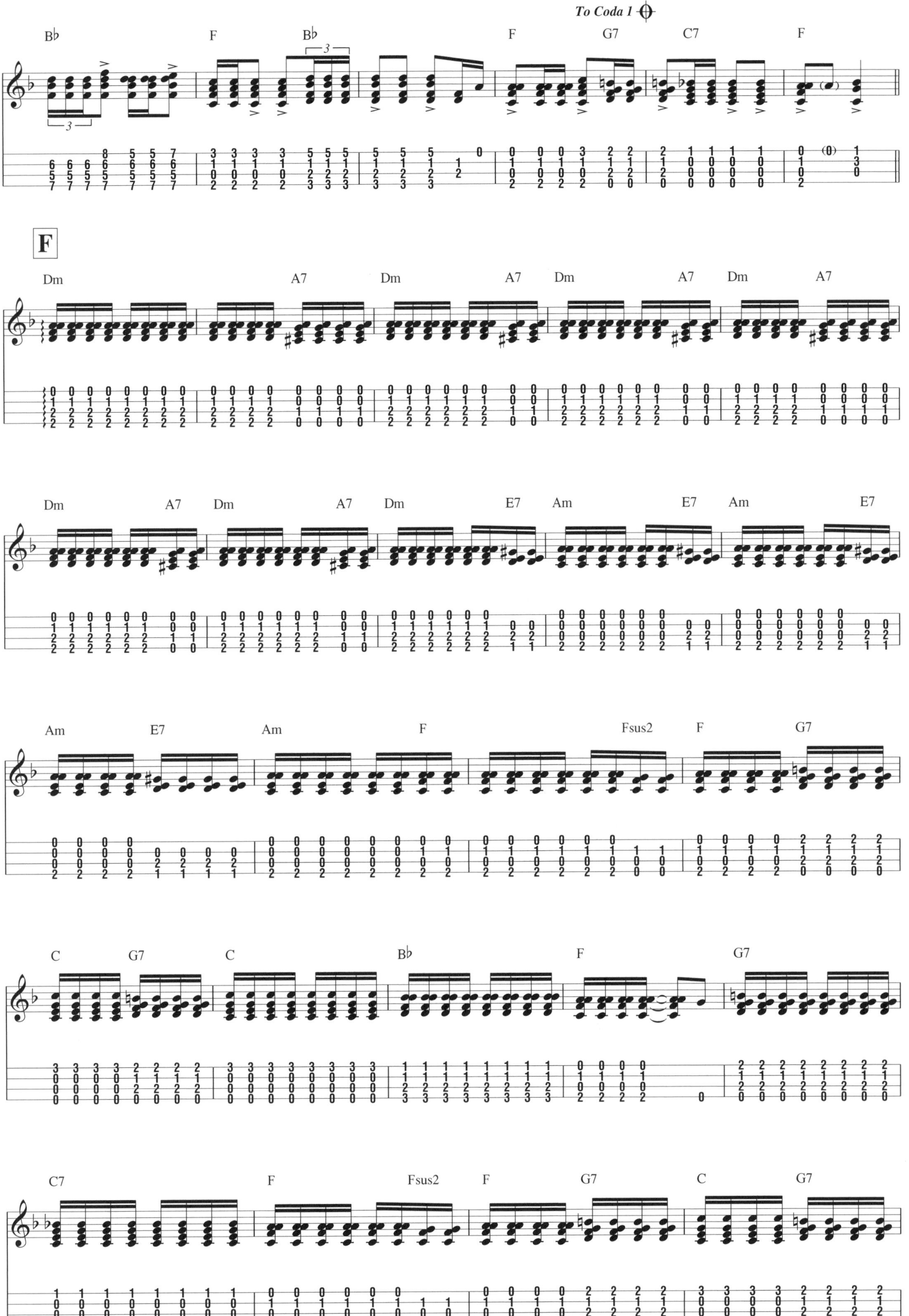

To Coda 1
B♭
F
B♭
F
G7
C7
F
F
Dm
A7
Dm
A7
Dm
A7
Dm
A7
Dm
A7
Dm
A7
Dm
E7
Am
E7
Am
E7
Am
E7
Am
F
Fsus2
F
G7
C
G7
C
B♭
F
G7
C7
F
Fsus2
F
G7
C
G7

D.S. al Coda 1

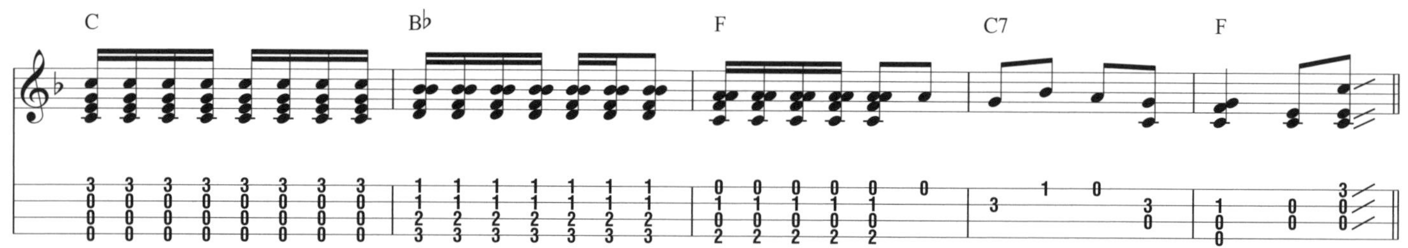
C
B♭
F
C7
F

Coda 1

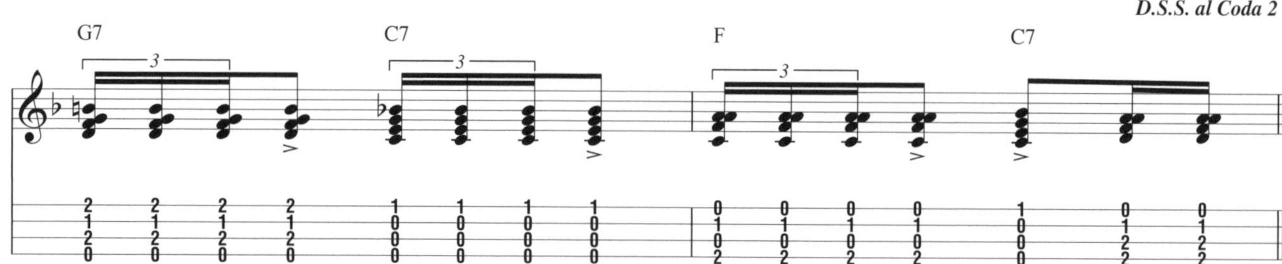
D.S.S. al Coda 2
G7
C7
F
C7

Coda 2

G

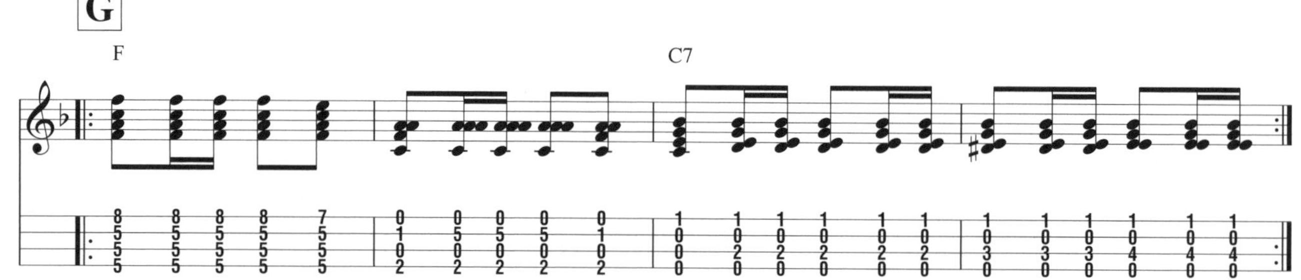
F
C7

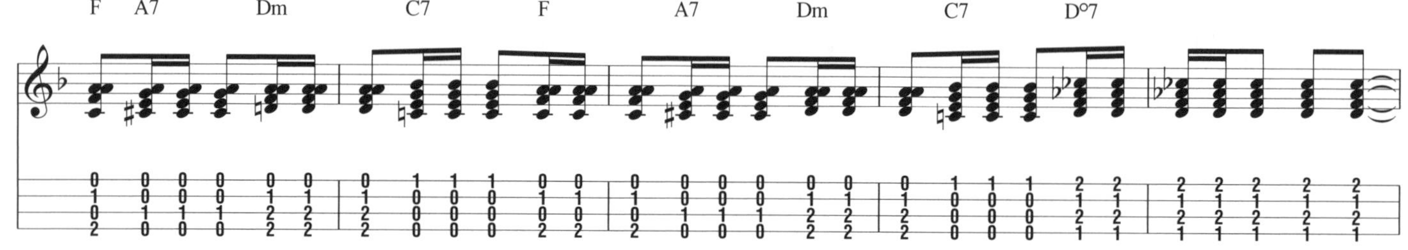
F
A7
Dm
C7
F
A7
Dm
C7
D°7

F
D♯°7

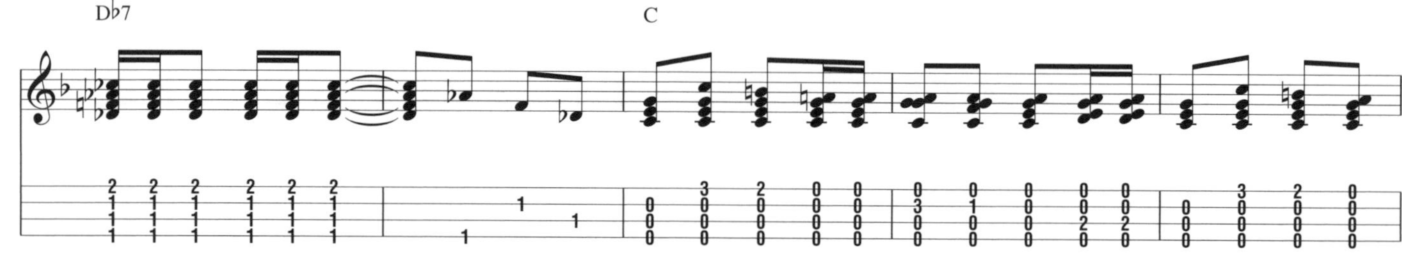
D♭7
C

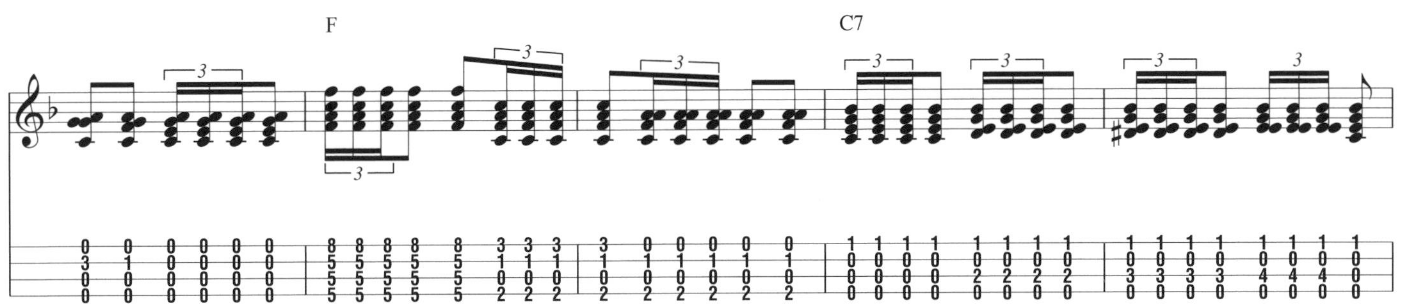
F
C7

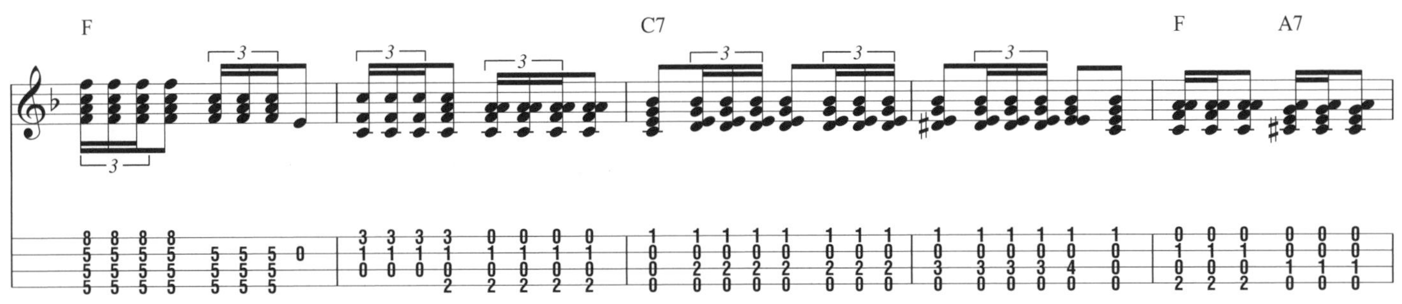
F
C7
F
A7

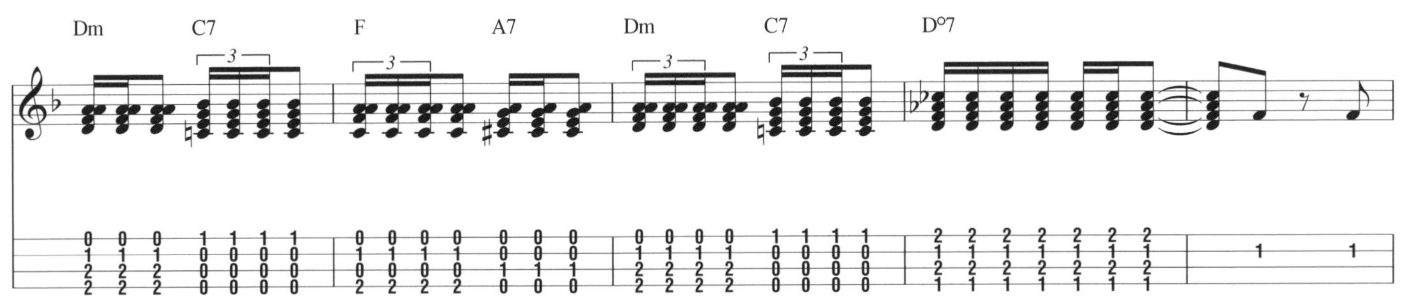
Dm
C7
F
A7
Dm
C7
D°7

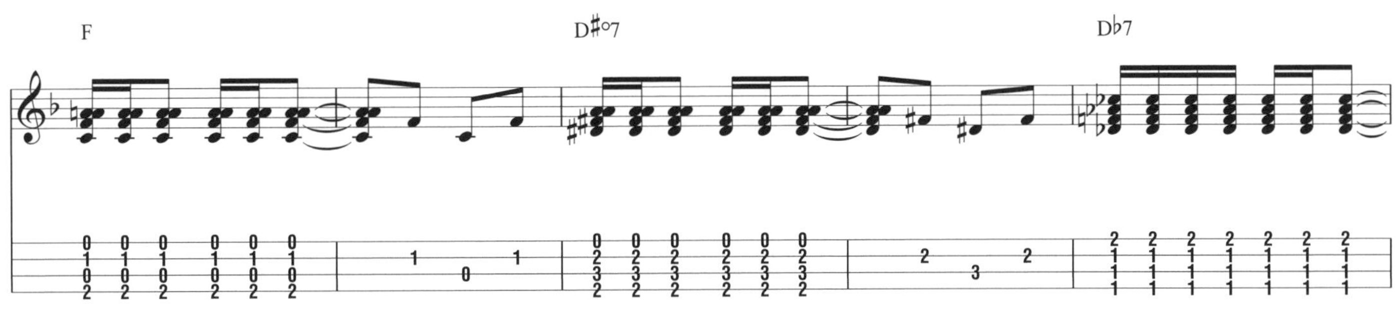
F
D♯°7
D♭7

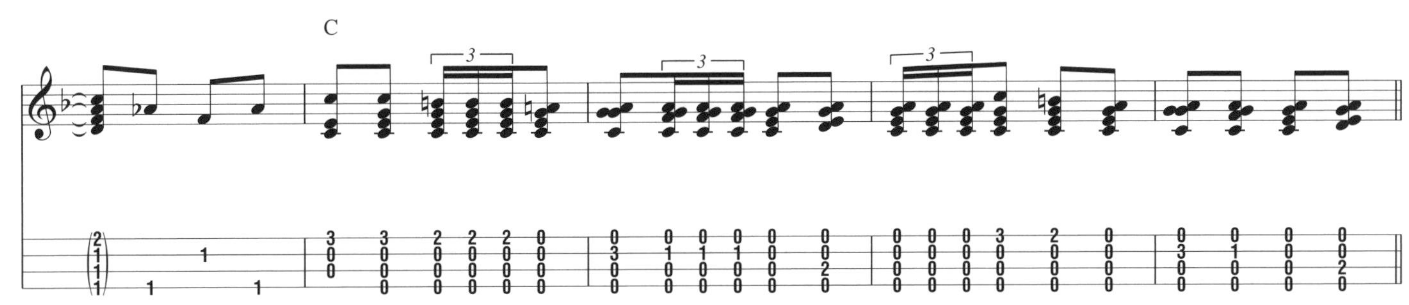
C

H

F C F

C F E F E F E

*Strum sixteenth-notes while sliding up.

F E F C

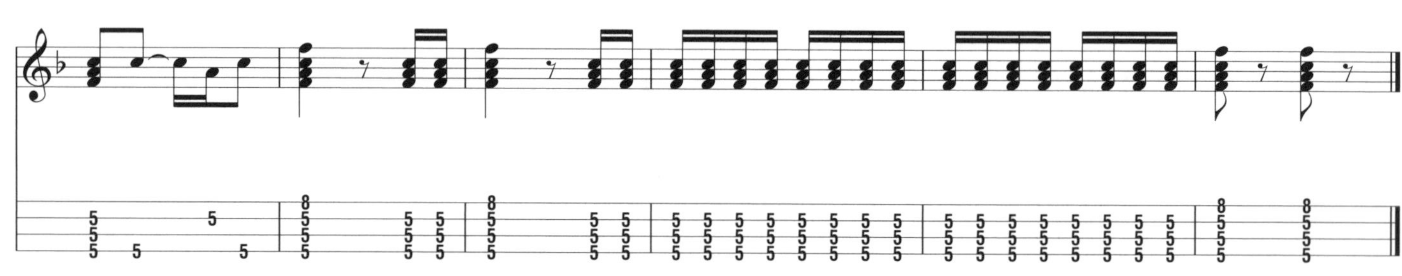

UKULELE NOTATION LEGEND

THE MUSICAL STAFF shows pitches and rhythms and is divided by bar lines into measures. Pitches are named after the first seven letters of the alphabet.

TABLATURE graphically represents the ukulele fingerboard. Each horizontal line represents a a string, and each number represents a fret.

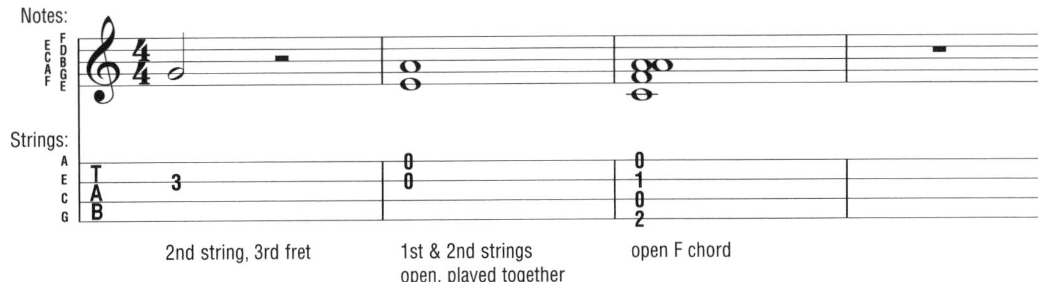

HALF-STEP BEND: Strike the note and bend up 1/2 step.

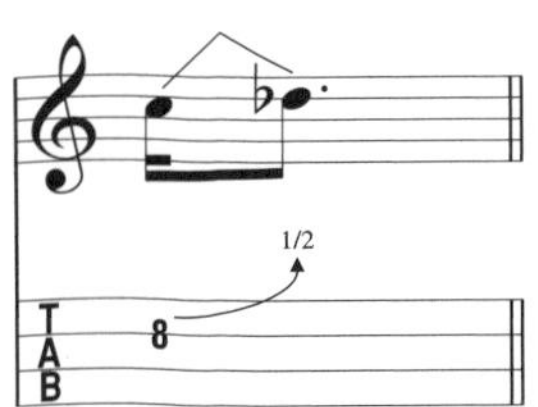

WHOLE-STEP BEND: Strike the note and bend up one step.

GRACE NOTE BEND: Strike the note and immediately bend up as indicated.

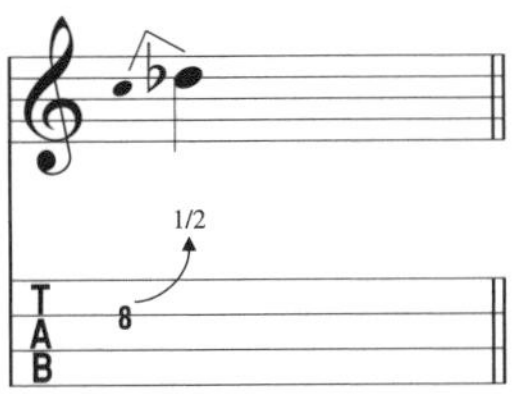

SLIGHT (MICROTONE) BEND: Strike the note and bend up 1/4 step.

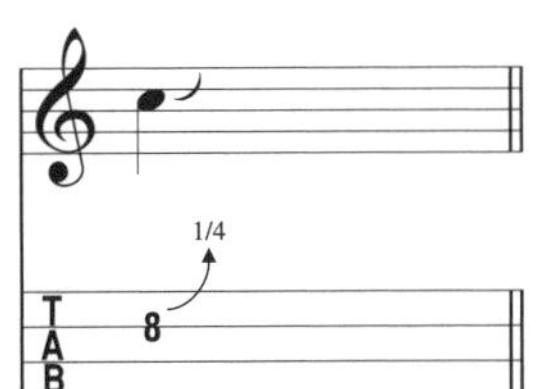

BEND AND RELEASE: Strike the note and bend up as indicated, then release back to the original note. Only the first note is struck.

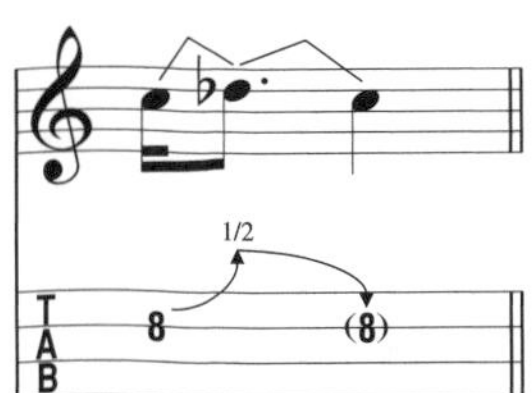

PRE-BEND: Bend the note as indicated, then strike it.

VIBRATO: The string is vibrated by rapidly bending and releasing the note with the fretting hand.

HAMMER-ON: Strike the first (lower) note with one finger, then sound the higher note (on the same string) with another finger by fretting it without picking.

PULL-OFF: Place both fingers on the notes to be sounded. Strike the first note and without picking, pull the finger off to sound the second (lower) note.

LEGATO SLIDE: Strike the first note and then slide the same fret-hand finger up or down to the second note. The second note is not struck.

SHIFT SLIDE: Same as legato slide, except the second note is struck.

TRILL: Very rapidly alternate between the notes indicated by continuously hammering on and pulling off.

TREMOLO PICKING: The note is picked as rapidly and continuously as possible.

NOTE: Tablature numbers in parentheses mean:

1. The note is being sustained over a system (note in standard notation is tied), or
2. The note is sustained, but a new articulation (such as a hammer-on, pull-off, slide or vibrato) begins, or
3. The note is a barely audible "ghost" note (note in standard notation is also in parentheses).

Additional Musical Definitions

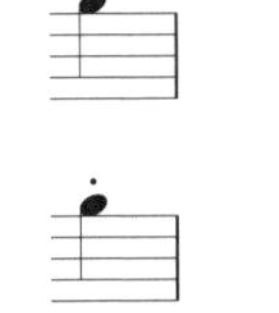

(accent) • Accentuate note (play it louder)

(staccato) • Play the note short

D.S. al Coda • Go back to the sign (𝄋), then play until the measure marked "***To Coda***," then skip to the section labelled "**Coda.**"

D.C. al Fine • Go back to the beginning of the song and play until the measure marked "***Fine***" (end).

N.C. • No chord.

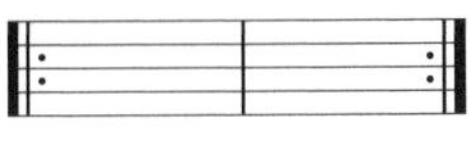

• Repeat measures between signs.

1. | 2.

• When a repeated section has different endings, play the first ending only the first time and the second ending only the second time.

HAL•LEONARD UKULELE PLAY-ALONG®

Now you can play your favorite songs on your uke with great-sounding backing tracks to help you sound like a bona fide pro!

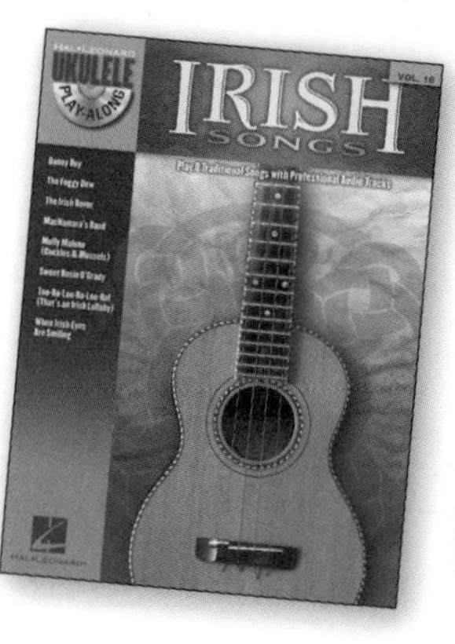

1. POP HITS
00701451 Book/CD Pack........................$14.99

2. UKE CLASSICS
00701452 Book/CD Pack........................$12.99

3. HAWAIIAN FAVORITES
00701453 Book/CD Pack........................$12.99

4. CHILDREN'S SONGS
00701454 Book/CD Pack........................$12.99

5. CHRISTMAS SONGS
00701696 Book/CD Pack........................$12.99

6. LENNON & MCCARTNEY
00701723 Book/CD Pack........................$12.99

7. DISNEY FAVORITES
00701724 Book/CD Pack........................$12.99

8. CHART HITS
00701745 Book/CD Pack........................$14.99

9. THE SOUND OF MUSIC
00701784 Book/CD Pack........................$12.99

10. MOTOWN
00701964 Book/CD Pack........................$12.99

11. CHRISTMAS STRUMMING
00702458 Book/CD Pack........................$12.99

12. BLUEGRASS FAVORITES
00702584 Book/CD Pack........................$12.99

13. UKULELE SONGS
00702599 Book/CD Pack........................$12.99

14. JOHNNY CASH
00702615 Book/CD Pack........................$14.99

15. COUNTRY CLASSICS
00702834 Book/CD Pack........................$12.99

16. STANDARDS
00702835 Book/CD Pack........................$12.99

17. POP STANDARDS
00702836 Book/CD Pack........................$12.99

18. IRISH SONGS
00703086 Book/CD Pack........................$12.99

19. BLUES STANDARDS
00703087 Book/CD Pack........................$12.99

20. FOLK POP ROCK
00703088 Book/CD Pack........................$12.99

21. HAWAIIAN CLASSICS
00703097 Book/CD Pack........................$12.99

23. TAYLOR SWIFT
00704106 Book/CD Pack........................$14.99

24. WINTER WONDERLAND
00101871 Book/CD Pack........................$12.99

7777 W. BLUEMOUND RD. P.O. BOX 13819 MILWAUKEE, WI 53213

www.halleonard.com

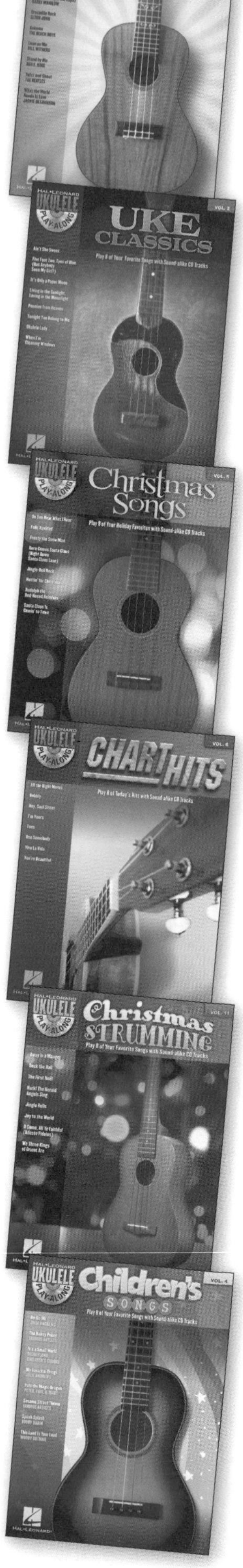

Prices, contents, and availability subject to change without notice.

0313